Creative Nonfiction

G. Douglas Atkins, *Series Editor*

For Bill and Willadene —
Friends and fellow
peaceniks — hope you like
these stories.
Jeff Gundy
12/95

A Community of Memory

A Community of Memory ∞

My Days with George and Clara

Jeff Gundy

University of Illinois Press

Urbana and Chicago

Library of Congress Cataloging-in-Publication Data

Gundy, Jeffrey Gene, 1952–
A community of memory : my days with George and Clara / Jeff Gundy.
p.   cm. — (Creative nonfiction)
ISBN 0-252-06496-8 (pbk. : alk. paper)
1. Mennonites—Illinois—Genealogy. 2. Gundy, George Ilive,
1880–1951—Family. 3. Gundy, Clara Strubhar, 1885–1979—Family.
4. Gundy family. 5. Strubhar family. 6. Illinois—Genealogy.
I. Title. II. Series.
F550.M45G86   1995
929'.2'0882870773—dc20   95-8456
                                                                      CIP

Contents

Illustrations follow page 70.

Partial Genealogy of the Gundy Family

Note: Names in boldface indicate speakers in this book.

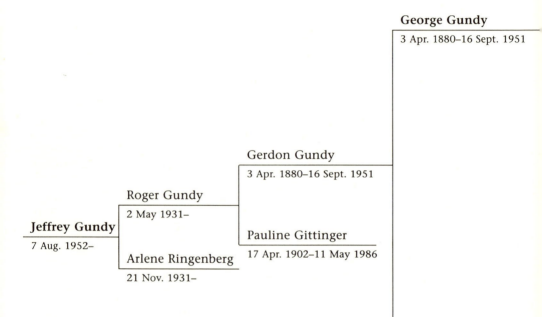

George Gundy
3 Apr. 1880–16 Sept. 1951

Gerdon Gundy
3 Apr. 1880–16 Sept. 1951

Roger Gundy
2 May 1931–

Jeffrey Gundy
7 Aug. 1952–

Pauline Gittinger
17 Apr. 1902–11 May 1986

Arlene Ringenberg
21 Nov. 1931–

Clara Strubhar
28 Jan. 1885–26 Feb. 1979

Barbara Gundy
15 Mar. 1820–15 Dec. 1893

John Gundy
1791(?)–1856–59

Jacob Gundy
26 Nov. 1846–26 Apr. 1919

Mary Schwartzentruber Birckelbaw
11 Oct. 1804–5 Mar. 1892

Michael Kinsinger
10 Oct. 1814–29 July 1895

Magdalena Kinsinger
11 Oct. 1804–5 May 1892

Peter Nafziger
23 Feb. 1789–16 Sept. 1885

Magdalena Nafziger
13 Mar. 1818–9 Aug. 1895

Barbara Beck
1 June 1790–4 Sept. 1865

Joseph Joder
13 Sept. 1797–31 Dec. 1887

Peter Strubhar
1770–21 Aug. 1835

John Strubhar
14 Oct. 1808–17 Nov. 1883

Peter Strubhar II
12 Nov. 1827–22 Oct. 1902

Marie Gerber
1782–27 Oct. 1864

Valentine Strubhar II
23 Apr. 1859–28 July 1941

Barbara Sweitzer
2 Feb. 1831–23 Aug. 1912

John Sweitzer
15 Sept. 1807–28 Jan. 1885

John Guth
20 Mar. 1840–2 Oct. 1896

Katherine Guth
21 Feb. 1865–8 Mar. 1941

Mary Engel
1 Dec. 1807–17 Feb. 1888

Mary Ehresman
8 Nov. 1839–8 Mar. 1894

Acknowledgments

This book would have been impossible without many sorts of help from many different people. The Bluffton College Study Center provided crucial financial support for the project and an audience for drafts of several chapters. Hilda Troyer did invaluable research on George and Clara and their relatives and ancestors, physical and otherwise, and passed it along to me. Steven R. Estes provided many rich glimpses of Illinois Mennonite history, both in his written histories of the North Danvers and Meadows Mennonite Churches and through letters and phone conversations. I made repeated use of Paton Yoder's translation of the minutes of the *Dienerversammlungen,* Willard Smith's voluminous and thorough *Mennonites in Illinois* (Scottdale, Pa.: Herald Press, 1983), and Olynthus Clark's "Joseph Joder, Schoolmaster-Farmer and Poet 1797–1887," which can be found in *Transactions of the Illinois State Historical Society* 36 (1929): 135–65. I also relied heavily on family histories by Vera Maud Sakemiller Root, *The Jacob and Magdalena Kinzinger Gundy Family* (1981), and by Christian W. Imhoff, *Peter Strubhar II Family Record* (1987).

Mary Bertsche and Harry Yoder let me visit them for interviews that became a pleasure as well as providing valuable information. Christian Imhoff helped identify photos, reminisced, and sent a copy of Valentine Strubhar's autobiography. Clarence Oyer, Claude Esch, Ralph Streid, and many others talked with me on various occasions. Peter Ropp and his son Ron were helpful and gracious, even though their ancestors do not fare especially well within these pages. Ann Hilty of the C. Henry Smith Mennonite Historical Library and Howard Raid of the General Conference Mennonite Archives, both in Bluffton, were generous with their time, materials, and expertise. Denny

Weaver's intricate knowledge of Mennonite history, theology, and politics, and his general encouragement regarding my investigation of things Mennonite, have meant a great deal to me over the years. Scott Russell Sanders, Mary Ann Sullivan, Roger Mitchell, and Julia Kasdorf also read drafts of various sections of the project, providing advice and feedback without which I'd have been lost, but which I fear all too often I have ignored, misunderstood, or just failed to accomplish. Stephen Corey and the *Georgia Review* provided support and invaluable editing advice for the essay out of which this project grew.

Then there are my uncles and aunts: Gerdon Gundy made copies of letters, John Gundy loaned me many old photographs, his wife, Jan, copied Clara's huge scrapbook for me, and Rev. James Gundy passed along a shoebox full of George's sermon notes. All of them, my uncle Dick, and many other family members shared stories and reflections with me, and Clara's diaries came to me from somewhere, too. To my parents, Roger and Arlene Gundy, I owe a debt beyond calculation, but here I must, at least, thank them for keeping the family history a living presence in my mind and spirit. And my wife, Marlyce, has—remarkably—put up with my absences, sulks, preoccupations, and pontifications and often served as first reader, all without leaving town. To her, again, my thanks.

I am grateful for permission to quote from "Meditation at Lagunitas" from *Praise* by Robert Hass. (c) 1974, 1975, 1976, 1977, 1978, 1979 by Robert Hass. First published by the Ecco Press in 1979. Reprinted by permission.

Earlier versions of parts of the preface, chapter 8, and the coda appeared in *Georgia Review* under the title "The Fact of Community: My Days with George and Clara." Another part of chapter 8 appeared in *Image: A Journal of the Arts and Religion* under the title "In Search of George and Clara." An earlier version of the second half of chapter 7 appeared in *Mennonite Life* under the title "Comets and Calls: From the Life of Valentine Strubhar." Chapter 4, in slightly different form, appeared in *Proceedings of the Conference Tradition and Transition: An Amish Mennonite Heritage of Obedience, 1693–1993*, ed. V. Gordon Oyer (Metamora: Illinois Mennonite Historical and Genealogical Society, 1994).

Preface

Rev. George Gundy, one of the pioneer preachers of the
Central Conference of Mennonites, passed to his eternal reward September 16, 1951. . . . Some one has said, "he who
is conscious of a debt he can never pay, will be forever paying it." And so we are greatly indebted to our brethren who
have gone before, and it brings to us the sobering sense of
responsibility for those who are gone as well as for those
who are to come.

—Rev. William B. Weaver, "In Memoriam"

Clara Gundy, you are a saint!

—Hilda Troyer, ca. 1976

And so we put them in the ground, and all that remained
were the stories. A few were told over and over, right and wrong, until
the retellings lay tangled in a nest of mainly well-meant misrepre-
sentations of whatever the pure events might once have been. Some
were only heard once or twice, casually at the dinner table or low in
the front seats of cars sliding through the dark along the roads George
loved to drive, fast. Some had nothing to do with them at all, except to fill in the depths of the history from which they had come,
the country their ancestors had shaped and struggled with, wrangling
and settling with the land, with each other, with whatever they chose
to think of as their souls, with their personal and corporate versions
of the one true God.

When I began in the summer of 1990 to explore the lives of my
ancestors on my father's side, Walt Whitman and Emily Dickinson
seemed more modern and more real to me than my own great-grand-

parents. I had pored over the poets' words again and again, read the lavished attention of critics and biographers, worried their smallest phrases, and speculated about the most obscure events of their lives. Like most teaching poets, I had spent far more time learning about writers than about my blood relatives. Clara Strubhar Gundy, my father's father's mother, I knew only as a tall, gaunt, grand old lady, and I had only pictures and stories of her husband, George; he died in 1951, a year before I became their first great-grandchild.

George Ilive Gundy was born in 1880 near Carlock, Illinois; one of the minor puzzles about him is his odd middle name, which no one has been able to account for. Clara Louise Strubhar was five years younger, the daughter of a prominent minister and farmer in nearby Washington. Both came from Amish-Mennonite families whose members originated in Switzerland and, after some time in France and Germany, came to America in the 1820s and 1830s, seeking good land and religious freedom. Their ancestors spent time in Ohio and, in George's case, Iowa before settling in the growing Amish-Mennonite community of central Illinois. Like most early settlers, they farmed and raised large families; they were plain in dress, German in speech, pacifist and communitarian in principle, a temperate and industrious people who quickly prospered in their modest way. In the last third of the nineteenth century they moved away from Amish restrictions on dress and technology, so that even George's parents' wedding picture from 1869 shows his father in a wide-lapeled suit and his mother in a showy dress with diamond earrings.

George and Clara themselves seemed the sort of ancestors we all wish for—upright, firm, and brave in the old brown photos. Relatives and aged friends still remembered them fondly. Although George and Clara weren't known outside the little farm towns in Illinois where they lived and the small group of Amish-Mennonite churches to which they belonged and in which George preached all his life, a little digging around taught me that they were still much more solidly in the world than I had expected. From one uncle I got a shoebox full of George's sermon notes; from another came Clara's diaries—kept from 1936 well into the 1970s—and photocopies of a huge scrapbook. A capable centennial history of the church in Meadows, Illinois, with a generous chapter on George's twenty-five years as pastor there, happened out in June. The wife of his successor at Meadows had worked for years on a biography of George and Clara, and she gave me a whole shopping bag full of notes, clippings, letters, and drafts, some of them going back to the start of the Anabaptist Reformation in 1525. I conducted interviews and had conversations that provided anecdotes and impressions, even the repetitive ones revealing. Many records of their churches are stored in the General Conference Mennonite Archives at Bluffton College, where I teach, and digging through them I found minutes and letters about George's pastoral duties, a few scraps of his own correspondence, and then another bundle of his sermons, misfiled under someone else's name.

And so I learned that they were far from dim ghosts, that they were gone but not silent nor invisible, that the ignorance was mine. I spent some time reading what I had about them, I wrote an essay about them, and then the summer was over and my hectic teaching schedule resumed. But I knew that my time with them wasn't finished. The next summer I got out all my notes again and decided to put together a brief sketch of *their* ancestors, starting with the first ones to come across the water. A few days, a week at most, I told myself. Just the main facts.

It took me two years to work my way back to George and Clara. I soon found out that no history is just one story, and the ones that led up to George and Clara's had their own fascinations. There were voices there that wanted to speak, that took on lives of their own as I tried to listen to them, to fill in their blanks. Their lives, as I pieced them together from family histories, scattered references, and general background reading, were both distinct and representative. Without being exceptional, they reflected and refracted the larger national and religious streams in which they moved. Most of the voices were relatives, direct or indirect, but when I came upon the story of Joseph Joder, schoolteacher, farmer, poet, and earnest heretic, I knew that he needed to be a part of this book too, even though he was merely a neighbor and fellow churchgoer—for a while—of my blood relations.

These stories are piecework. As much as possible they describe what "really" happened, patched and filled and stretched where the details are lost or the narrative seemed to demand some invention. The people in them are all connected in some way to George and Clara, and through them to me; so are dozens and hundreds of others, of course, but I heard these few speaking, not always clearly, but firmly, as though they were reconciled to dying but not to letting their stories die out.

The people in this book are gone and I am still here, and if I take advantage of the power that gives me it is not because I mean to disgrace or disservice them. Nor do I mean this to be one more set of quaint anecdotes about the simple but noble ancestors. It's my failing, but it has taken me far longer than it should have to recognize that while the people in these pages mostly lived before flush toilets, computerized dashboards, and routine postsecondary education, they were neither stupid nor simple. Most of them, anyway.

I have the blood in my veins, a mildly obsolete but functional computer and adequate typing skills, a box full of notes and copies from three summers of research, and a list of addresses and phone numbers I can turn to when facts elude me. They have their whole lives, silent and vanished now, but each of them ten or seventy or ninety years of days and months and seasons, meals and work and loving and grieving and trips to the outhouse or the bathroom—myriad lifetimes of inner monologues whose contents remain only in the mind of God. What is here is not complete, not satisfactory, not to be trusted, but it's what I, with the help of all these others living and dead, have been able to do.

ONE ∽

Half a World Away:
John Strubhar, 1837

I didn't mind the work so much, really. It kept me from too much sampling of the whiskey, that's for certain. I did get plenty tired by the end of the week, doing my own work and the head distiller's too, as I did for those two years after he took sick. The bed I slept on did not get much turning, and some of those winter days I barely saw the sun. But of course Brother Christian Augspurger, being a good man of the church as well as the second or third richest Christian in Hamilton County, with his land and his mills and distilleries and his fancy stone house he called "Chrisholm" like some baron in the old country, would never hear of work on Sunday, so there was that relief. Still, on the Sundays we had preaching, more than half of the day was taken up with meeting, which would have gone better by my lights if the benches had backs on them, so at least a man could rest a little while the preacher was somewhere in the prophets. But that would be worldliness, I suppose, and with the Hessians moving in with their carpets and pianos and fancy buttons we had already enough arguing about worldliness to last me a lifetime.

The years I worked double came before I bought the farm in Illinois, paid for in cash and the deed in my hand, all those hours made into real earth and trees and crops to come, or so I hoped. By the time Mutti and the rest arrived in 1837, though, I could hardly remember what it looked like. Half my time I spent trying to remember it, the way the land rolled down to the creek under the trees, the patch around the cabin that Beech and his sons had cleared while they squatted on it and which no doubt was growing back over deeper and thicker every spring, the big dead trees they'd girdled and planted their corn around, felling them for firewood or when they had the ambition left at the end of a day. And the little dark cabin that I spent one night in before starting the long walk back—dirt floor, string latch, two little windows with only shutters, no glass, the whole thing overrun by the squirrels and insects so that the outside could hardly have been dirtier. Nothing to write home about, surely, but of course I wrote about it anyway and didn't stretch things much, only to tell them it was a start and the land was good and as soon as I could raise the fares we'd see it together.

Mutti was not quite so eager to leave Alsace. There was all her family around her, and she never liked the water, and she didn't quite see what the fuss was either about a new place and new land, more than anyone could ever own, there to be taken. It was Vater's dream really, to have land for all his sons and to be able to live together with our own people and gather for worship every Sunday instead of being scattered around the countryside. Of course there was also the problem of finding land enough to keep a family alive, let alone get ahead at all, and when on top of all else the talk began of the new French government making all the young men do their time in the army, Mutti stopped digging in her heels. Before I left she told me that she prayed to God we would all greet each other in America, but if not at least she would know that her first son would not be aiming a gun at some other mother's son.

I was just eighteen in 1826 when they sent me over. Those first days on the boat I was lonely and frightened enough to last my whole life, and then sick too, until I wished to die just to lie quiet, and I thought more than once that the grave could hardly be more cramped and filled with stench than the steerage of the boat, crammed with four other young men into a cubicle we could barely sit up or lie down in, let alone stand. And the welcome at Castle Garden in New York was not so warm either, with the crowds and the endless waiting in line for one stranger after another to ask their cross questions in English. I had only the few words I'd picked up on the boat, but I made it through and kept my trunk out of the hands of the villains on the docks, who preyed on anyone just off the boats. It helped greatly to have the letters from the Augspurgers, telling what to beware of and how to find the canal boat west and then the stage to Pittsburgh and then on down the river to Cincinnati. Young as I was the sharpers came around me almost as bad as the mosquitoes, thinking to swindle me one way or another, but I kept my wits about me and the little money I had hidden safe in my shoe. The river boat had an English sign that someone told me said not to turn in with my boots on, but I did anyway, and got through safe and sound.

Once I made my way to Ohio the living settled down a good bit. It was just six months after I started working for Christian Augspurger that his head distiller took sick, and though it took some talking to persuade him to let me try both jobs for double the pay, he finally agreed to give me a chance. As hard as I worked, there were days I might just as well have been back home, working in the distillery and coming home too tired for anything but a quick bite before prayers and bed. Of course I missed the family and the old home place, with all of us gathered about the table on Sunday. But when I got lonesome, I would just think of the money in the mattress and how soon there would be enough for them all to come over and eat together right here in Ohio.

There were a good number of our folk around Trenton, twenty families at least from Alsace, and the land there was very fine. I'd have been happy enough to settle there for life, but all the best land was taken up already and selling for a price too dear for a poor boy like me to get more than enough to put a garden on. Just after I bought the farm in Illinois, $350 for eighty acres and a house (all right, a cabin, and miserable enough), Christian Iutzi paid $25 an acre for good river bottom land near Trenton. And even before then, of course, the Hessian Mennonites had started moving in too, buying up land besides stirring up trouble with their buttons and pianos. Some of them were good men, like the preacher Peter Nafziger, who so loved to travel and serve God he was scarcely home enough to greet his wife, much less plant his corn. He was always off on some trip to Illinois or Iowa or Kentucky or Pennsylvania or even New Orleans, where he walked twice, though anyone reasonable would have taken the boat. He came to Ohio two years earlier than me, in 1828, and was our preacher for a while when he was somewhere in the county, but when he was so often gone off somewhere we chose Jacob Augspurger, Christian's second cousin, to minister too.

Brother Peter, everyone called him the Apostle because of his travels, had been in Canada with the Goldsmiths and some others. They decided after a few cold years that the rest could freeze their toes off up there without them. And as I say, most of the Hessians, some of them from Canada and some straight from Germany, were good men and women all told. Only they were not quite so strict as those of us from Alsace and not quite what we expected either when they started to move in with their big trunks and baggage. They wore fancy buttons on their clothes instead of sober hooks and eyes, put carpets and frilly curtains in their houses, and the Iutzis even brought a piano over with them and wanted to use it during services. Some said they were even teaching their children to play worldly songs and sing in parts. It caused plenty of talking, that I can tell you, until finally we had a big meeting and decided the Hessians should make their own congregation and the rest of us our own, with Peter Nafziger the minister for the Hessians and Jacob Augspurger and Peter Schrock for us. That was in 1835 as I remember, and after that things went smoother, but mostly I had too much work to do to get all excited about it.

So I figured if Canada was too cold for the Hessians it was too cold for me. And there were plenty of stories of the wonderful land to the west to be had almost for the taking. Some pamphlets made Illinois out to be so rich a man could just throw down the seed and then jump back so it didn't take him up with it into the sky, and those I didn't take too serious of course. But also I talked with the people passing through, and lots of them there were with the whiskey business going so big. I heard more than one driver talk of the big prairies of Illinois, so wide they were like the ocean, and the rich land along the creeks and rivers with plenty of trees and water and good fishing too, and that in the middle of the state—just west and a little north from us—there was still plenty of land and nobody much to claim it. So I started to think, na, maybe that's the place for us. Finally I decided at least to go see for myself.

And such a trip I had to get there, too. I had thought myself used to America, so big and empty of people, but I didn't know what big and empty was until I went up to Richmond and started west across Indiana. To save time walking I headed straight west; there were some of our people already to the north in Indiana, but they were far out of my path. Two days I walked and never saw another person nor a trace of one, only the bush and the Indian trail I followed. I knew there were Indians still around but not one nor any smoke nor a dead fire even did I see besides my own, not that I was so eager to meet them, mind you. Not even a bear or a wolf, though crossing more than one creek I found signs of them. Smaller game there was and plenty, so that just holding my rifle and keeping an eye out I never lacked for fresh meat. But except for the trail there was nothing to show that another man had ever passed over the ground.

By noon of the second day I felt half convinced I was Adam, just awakened to discover the Garden. Only this was bigger and grander and wilder than any garden you've ever seen, with the birds and the insects so loud in the trees sometimes that I thought they would make me deaf. Early enough in the spring it was that the mosquitoes and flies were not bad, and the walking was easy enough except for the swamps and sloughs everywhere, so that my boots were always wet through, and halfway up my legs too. I kept a sharp eye for snakes but saw only a few and had to kill none.

Late on the third day I broke out of the woods and looked down a long, slight slope of grass, not tall yet but shifting in the wind. There were little groves here and there, trees and brush scattered off in the distance, and a few deer nibbling at new shoots and the sun going down in front of me, a little stream on one side and from the trees I guessed a fair-sized river off in the distance. And so I stopped and looked at it all for a minute, spread out before me like the Promised Land, and I could almost not breathe so calm and quiet and beautiful it all was, and me here all alone, the only human being there to see it. I felt small as an ant or a field mouse then, out there with only a trail I did not quite trust and a gun and a sack with a blanket and some cornmeal and salt in it, the rabbit that I'd shot two hours ago cooling on my shoulder, with more of God's great wild earth than it seemed any man could see and still hope to live all around me, spreading out in every direction. I felt my feet were barely touching the ground, and my whole body seemed light and airy as a feather, such a tiny thing in all this place so still and green and beautiful, and I thought how great a God it must take to hold it all in His hand.

So I stopped then, made a fire by the stream, let some water settle in the pot and drank my fill, and made a stew with the rabbit. And I sat there with the night coming on and my belly full and money in my purse, going toward a place that I had never seen but where the Lord willing my family would make a new home. So solemn and full it all seemed to me, like my brain was getting bigger inside my head, thinking of all that was going on that I was part of, and the others depending on me only to settle whether it all went well or bust, and how if I were to lose my way or break an ankle out here I would end my days a hundred miles from any man and half a world away from Mutti and Vater and the rest, and they never to hear what had become of me or know where my bones were resting. And even with a few sips on the little whiskey bottle I brought for snakebite and emergencies I lay long and long awake in my blanket that night, hearing every small noise in the dark woods.

The next morning I went on, tired as I was, and about midday I came to the Wabash River and found the little settlement at Terre

Haute easily enough. They pointed me on to the west and then I really saw prairies; the next day I walked four hours without seeing a tree, and the sun already hot enough too, but a wind in my face helped a little. So I found my way, following the streams when I could for the shade of the trees, and finally I made it to Mackinawtown on the river, which someone had told me was the county seat. Not so much of a town it was either, but in the first tavern I went into for a bite and some news I met a man named Beech, who said he had built a house and a barn and cleared some land on Rock Creek not so far away. "Five dollars an acre for it all," he said, "eighty prime acres but I cannot stay, the neighbors are getting too close on all sides. I've said ever since I got my growth that when someone else's axe wakes me of a morning it's time to move on."

Well, I knew at once this Beech was not my sort, and five dollars was more than I had money for, but I told him I would look at it. So next morning he led me off into the wilderness and a half-day's trudge over trails and traces that were rough enough on foot and would have bogged or broken any wagon I'd ever seen, bragging all the time about how of the seven houses between Blooming Grove and Mackinawtown his was the finest of them all. And at last there was his place, near a little creek and in a good stand of timber, though if it was the finest I was not anxious to see the others. He had girdled trees to kill them but grubbed out only the smaller ones, and huge dead oaks and maples stood gaunt as old men everywhere. Underneath them the weeds and trash and deadwood were doing a long ways better than the corn, which was just poking up where he'd planted it, looking sickly and about to give it up already. And Beech had given up too on the whole business, I could see, and not bothered to plant the rest nor to weed any of it. The cabin, as I said, was nothing much either, and the barn just the roughest of sheds to keep the one cow he had from freezing in the blizzards. I knew that he'd paid not a nickel for the land, but had just been squatting on it, hoping to raise the money to buy it when it came for sale from the government somehow or to find some fool like me with money to pay him for his improvements and take it off his hands.

Still, the longer I looked the more I liked the place. The creek seemed a good one, and the bluffs along it were high enough that the land would not flood too often. From the size of the weeds the soil must be decent enough, and the water I pulled up from the well smelled better than some. And I found myself imagining how it would look with the trees gone from the corn ground, with the cabin cleaned up and a room added on the back maybe, with a big garden. And if what he had done was sloppy and second-rate, still it was work that I and my brothers would not have to do. And I thought how much money I had and how long I had worked to save it, and I bit down hard once and then offered him four dollars an acre. He sputtered around for a while with more tales of his hard work and suffering, and I said that I understood all that but was not made of money either, and finally he said that for four-fifty it was mine.

So then it was the long trudge back to Trenton, and back to work, which was just as well as that winter was the worst anyone could remember in Ohio and even worse in Illinois, with three or four feet of snow on the ground from December to March and the people everywhere near to dying, but especially off in the brush five or six miles from town with the wolves howling and sniffing around outside, hungrier even than the people inside the cabins. People speak of it still. But it passed, though the next summer was a bad one too—a late spring and the corn nipped in the fall by a quick frost. Still, we got by, or most of us did. And I was too busy working and writing back to Mutti and Vater in what little time I had, and planning what all we could do when we were settled on the farm, to think too much even about what was right around me. Na, I did find myself sometimes stopping on the street to watch some fetching lady pass by, or gazing at the girls' row in the meeting much too long, and once or twice they caught me and set to giggling and whispering to each other. Some nights my bed in the little room I rented seemed just too cold and lonely to stand for another winter by myself. But I knew all that would have to wait. What a day it was when I went to Hamilton to get the bank draft and sealed the envelope and sent it off to France! Then it was the months of waiting and wondering if some thief would get all my hard-earned dollars or the boat would go down with them, or even worse the boat carrying Mutti and Vater and the rest to me.

It cracked my heart nearly to hear that Vater was dead, and from blood poisoning yet, skinning some rabbit or woodchuck he'd probably poached in the moonlight, as if he didn't know not to cut himself or if he did to go see the herb doctor before it started to get red and angry. When the letter came I was getting a wagon loaded for the trip to Cincinnati. Mail was not all so rare a thing then in Ohio, yet of course we were always excited by a letter from home, so I tore open the envelope smiling. But a grown man bawling his eyes out in the middle of the day made all the hands stop and gawk until finally I ran off into the woods and left the wagon to get loaded without me. So there I am in the dead of winter, with snow in my boots and the tears freezing on my cheeks, pushing through the drifts like some clumsy blubbering bear, and suddenly I wonder whether Mutti can get back the money for Vater's ticket. Such a terrible thing a mind is, na? My own father laid in the ground, and this is what I think about.

But God works in his ways, and what do we know. I already knew that my brother Joseph had married and with two small daughters thought it best not to come until later. And so it happens. Once you start in to leave the ones you love, to do what it seems is yours to do in this world, you don't know what will come between you nor if you'll ever meet again before you gather all at the river. And so Vater was gone and in the ground all these months already with me working away happy and whistling every day of it, thinking only of how soon I would see him and hug him close to me again.

With the mails so slow it was not long after the news about Vater that Mutti and the rest arrived. Such a great day it was when the wagon rolled into town and there was Mutti, and Magdalena and Valentine and Peter too. I was watching over the distillery that day, but I doused the fire and took the dogs off the treadmill and told someone that I was taking the day to be with my family just come from across the water, and anyone didn't like it could settle with me tomorrow.

How could I know my own brothers and sisters, it had been ten years you know, and little Peter was not even born when I left and now here he was half grown, not big but quick and hungry as an ox, trying to make up for the trip. For a funny moment I thought he was Valentine, who had been that size near enough when I left, and that he had not changed at all, only I had. But Mutti seemed the same almost, just a little gray and tired, as who would not be after their terrible crossing, and Magdalena my half sister from Vater's first marriage all a grown-up woman, tall and beautiful, and Valentine strong and calm and quiet. When we all sat down at table in the cabin I'd built once I knew they were coming it was like all those years were just a day, even if there was that place on the end where it seemed like Vater should come in from the washtrough and sit down to ask the blessing. I didn't want to but Mutti looked at me hard for a moment, and at last I sat down there and said, "Na, shall we pray?" And I thanked God for bringing us together again from so far apart and so long, and remembered Joseph and his family still on the other side of the water, and remembered Vater across the River Jordan and waiting there for us to join him. And I asked that he would hold us up and give us strength in this great new land and keep us well and faithful, all in Jesus' name, Amen. And we all snuffled a little before we turned to the meat and the corn dodgers and the coffee, and Mutti, who never cared who saw her cry, took out her hanky and wiped her eyes and said with almost a smile, "You could have said thanks that never again must we ride a boat across the ocean!"

They had such an awful trip on the boat, much worse than mine, first big storms and then no wind at all so they hung for days on the water with nothing in sight, nothing to do, toward the end nothing to eat but a biscuit a day. For all her worrying and fear of the water Mutti stood the voyage better than the boys, who were sick first and then after they got their sea legs restless and bored. On the short rations they got sick again toward the end, feverish, sluggish, and half wild by turns, crammed below decks in those suffocating compartments I myself remember sharp enough never to want to see or smell them again.

Of course this was Mutti's telling of it. Valentine claimed he had not been so bad but Peter was awful and Peter said it was Valentine who wanted to boil up Magdalena's shoes and eat them. Magdalena gave out with her beautiful big laugh and said they had both almost killed Mutti and her with worry, while all she had worried about was keeping some room between her and those sailors with their groping hands. Now shouldn't they be glad to be on dry land and under a family roof again, she said, with stew in the pot and meal on the shelf. And Valentine said ja, and more whiskey in town than a hundred Frenchmen could drink in a lifetime, and we all laughed. We had a little sip to celebrate, except for Peter of course, and then said another prayer to the great God for letting us sit here together again.

So it took more time then for us to be ready to move. With the fall well underway already and winter not so far off, Mutti was not about to leave Trenton, where we had at least a cabin and people around us for the wilds of Illinois, and the stories she heard about Indians and wolves and cougars settled her mind for sure. So Valentine got work at the distillery with me and we worked out the winter and got ready to leave as soon as the weather broke. I did ease back some on my work after they came, and of course Mutti and Lena were there to cook and clean, so it was a good bit more pleasant for me then. And yet so eager I was to be on my own land, answering to nobody but myself and God and away from the bickering over buttons and such and able to look for a wife to share my new home with me, that last winter was the hardest of all in some ways. But I told myself I had waited this long and could manage a little while more.

It was surely some work, trying to farm in the middle of the bush like that, especially remembering the land in Alsace, so long culti- vated and every corner smoothed out for the plow. But having not been worked for years the soil was plenty good, and the rains good too that first year, enough but not quite too much for the corn, so that even with our little plot we got what we needed to keep us go- ing and a little extra. The wheat and potatoes did well too, and with the game we ate high that winter—and of course there was plenty of wood for burning and building. Our people kept moving in near- by, so that by the springtime there were enough of us to gather for meeting every now and again, with Christian Ropp or Peter Farni preaching in somebody's house and the brethren from farthest away staying over in a barn if they needed to.

The Farnis had a store and a mill a few miles north of us on the Mackinaw, and the place was called Farnisville. Christian Ropp and Joseph Gingerich worked with them doing blacksmithing and cut- ting boards and grinding grain, and before long there was a regular little town there, or at least a place to get supplies and have the lit- tle work done that we could afford but couldn't do ourselves. Hard it was those first years to make any cash money, with corn sometimes only ten cents a bushel and no one to buy it anyway and the roads so bad we could hardly get it to Mackinawtown to send it downriv- er. I understood for sure then why the Augspurgers had started dis- tilling, and we tried a little of that, but mostly we got by without. We kept working on the roads, and little by little they got better, and then the railroad came in. By the time the Civil War came along lit- tle Peter was married to his Barbara and out on his own, and he bor- rowed money to buy his first big farm and the walnut grove too and we all thought he would go under for sure. But instead with the war the wheat price went crazy and he got, if not rich like the Augspurg- ers, still plenty comfortable. But that's yet to come.

Even those first hard years we did get around enough to see some of the brethren and sisters from farther away. I heard not long after we came that Anna Schertz, who had grown up close to us in France, was living with her family near Gridley, just northeast of us twenty miles or so. She was a girl only when I left, but one I still remem- bered, quick and light on her feet and clever too. Now she was all grown, not quite so quick perhaps but with eyes that made me not care about that or much of anything else. And so I went up to see her once or twice, though a long enough trip it was on a horse, and then asked Brother Christian Farni to go speak for me to her parents. He did and came back and said, yes, they agree, and so I was happy.

And then he said, "Na, John, one more thing while we are talking of marrying. Magdalena, she is your half sister only, and older than you, but would a person wanting to speak about her speak to your mother or you?" Poor Brother Christian, who was usually so sure of himself, and the richest of us on the Mackinaw for twenty miles each way, here he was stumbling like a schoolboy.

I said, "Na, I suppose being the man of the house I could hear such a speaking. But who might you be speaking for?" Of course I knew and everyone else too that Brother Christian had been eying Lena for a year and more, but for all his money he was shy a little with women and she certainly was not one to be taken lightly. His face went all red and his eyes went every which way around the room, as though he was following the flies.

"Na, John," he said finally, "you know I'm too old to be stuttering and stumbling this way and not be speaking for myself. Will she have me, do you think?" And of course she would, and of course I was not about to tell her nay. So we had two weddings in the family to take care of then, mine in December of 1839 and Magdalena's with Brother Christian early in the next year. And so we went on, poor as we were and the corn price always down and down if anyone wanted it at all, the bugs and the fevers plaguing us and more work to do in a day than any four men could manage. Still you know we were there, together mostly, and eating well and working for ourselves and worshipping with our own and no one to tell us different. And a worse life was not hard to remember.

And here we pause, having heard most of what anybody knows about the early days of John Strubhar and his kin in America, with additional information lifted from various other sources—and of course the sheer invention of a number of things. To this point, the things I don't know, though plentiful, have seemed minor enough not to cause too much worry. The dates of John's comings and goings and those of his family from Europe are perplexing, and just which year they all moved to Illinois is a matter of some confusion. But all that is mere history.

With the marriage business we enter another realm, the country of fiction, and the kind of lost story that fiction writers of the sort I am not make their livelihoods fleshing out or carving into novels of the sort this is not. Valentine Strubhar II's history of the Strubhar family says that in the spring of 1839 "Uncle John took another adventurous streak. With an ox team and a two-wheeled cart he drove to Gridley, Illinois and brought home a beautiful young bride in all the pomp and glory of those pioneer days in the person of Miss Anna Schertz." Esther Risser Leys's 1939 Strub-

har family history says that Anna was "also a native of Strasbourg, France, who came to America with her parents via New Orleans in 1831."

*But there is another story hinted at in Harry Weber's **Centennial History of the Mennonites of Illinois**. An appendix by Harold S. Bender says that according to Emil Mannhardt, "[John] Strupphar is said to have married Anna Schertz in 1839 after a licence had been issued to him and Elizabeth Landis. He is said to have arrived in Illinois unmarried, accompanied by several sisters, one of whom, Magdalena, was married to Christian Farney by John Nafziger in 1840."*

The plot thickens, does it not? Who was this Elizabeth Landis? It's a good Amish/Mennonite name, but no one bearing the family name, much less that particular name, is mentioned in Illinois by any of my histories until 1847, and then only in Sterling well to the north, and those Landises were members of the Reformed Mennonite church, a tiny sect of people unusually stubborn—even for Mennonites—who would have almost nothing to do with mainstream Mennonites and Amish, considering them "corrupt, worldly, and spiritually dead." I cannot find the name in Butler County, Ohio, either. There were plenty of Landis families in Pennsylvania, most of them mainline Mennonite rather than Amish, but how would John Strubhar, whose travels were limited almost entirely to those recounted here, have met someone clear out there, much less planned to marry her?

The story could be simply false, of course. Or she could be a mysterious stranger, the great love of his life, but doomed to be separated when their families found out, torn away and taken back to her own life before she had more than a glimpse of his. Was she a Lutheran or (even worse) a Catholic? Did she die young, like Lincoln's fabled Anne Rutledge? Did she break it off herself, run off with a French trapper, simply disappear? All this seems too romantic for the John Strubhar I know—but then how well do I know him?

About Anna Schertz I know little more, although if she indeed was from Strasbourg, John might well have known her there. According to Weber, David and Joseph Schertz came to Wesley City in Tazewell County in 1831, although he does not mention any female Schertzes, and Wesley City is west of John Strubhar's farm while Gridley is northeast. In fact it's odd that Anna would be in Gridley in 1839 at all, because the place was barely settled then; the main influx of people to the wide open prairie thereabouts did not start until the 1850s, when the prairies were being broken in earnest. Again, her name is not found in my histories outside of the brief mentions above, and her family connections remain a mystery. There were Schertzes in Butler County at least by 1835, when they joined with the Hessians who left the Augspurger hook-and-eye church, and so John also might have known Elizabeth from those days, if she and her family came from Butler County to Illinois as many others did.

It seems only natural that John would cast about for a wife as soon as practical after settling on the farm. He had postponed marriage for ten years longer than typical in his time; presumably he was, as a good Christian, secure in St. Paul's judgment that it is better to marry than to burn. But I find myself wanting to exert a completely irrelevant and inappropriate descendant's discretion and ask a few questions before he dashes into this. Just how well did he know this young woman, anyway? Could she cook? Could she clean? What's her name? Who's her daddy? Has he taken any time to show her what you need to live?

Of course I should quit confusing my tenses here. John Strubhar has already dashed into it, if lumbering toward Gridley behind a team of oxen can be called dashing, one hundred fifty-some years ago as I sit here typing this on a hot day in August in Bluffton, Ohio. He did marry and lived out a long life, siring ten children with Anna, never again leaving Illinois so far as I know. He was a charter member of the Yoder Meeting, which was formed in 1851 and became known as the Rock Creek church and then the North Danvers congregation. In 1860 he was ordained as deacon on the same day that Joseph Stuckey, soon to be known as the father of the Stuckey Amish, was ordained as preacher. In 1866 John Strubhar's barn was the site of the fifth **Dienerversammlung,** or ministers' meeting, of the Amish. His farm on Rock Creek was only a mile from the Rock Creek Meetinghouse, which was far too small to hold the crowds. On some days 1,500 people are said to have come for the preaching and, I suspect, the chance to socialize. He supported the development of free local schools as well as the church, and was known and respected throughout the community.

About forty miles from John's farm was Springfield and the law practice of Abraham Lincoln, whose family had moved to New Salem, Illinois, from Spencer County, Indiana, in the same year that John Strubhar bought his farm on Rock Creek and then walked back to work. Lincoln had also been busy in the meantime; he served briefly in the Black Hawk War of 1832, seeing no action, met and become friendly with Anne Rutledge (who died of malaria at the age of nineteen), read every book he could find, passed the bar in 1836, and then moved to Springfield to practice. He would later make the acquaintance of Joseph Joder, of Christian Farni, who married my four-times-great half aunt Magdalena Strubhar, and of other players in this story to be named later.

John Strubhar rarely spoke in public, but at the 1871 **Dienerversammlung** at Gridley Prairie, when the ministers were too divided even to discuss their differences openly and one after another were being called forth to deliver "admonitions" to fill up the time, he was called upon to speak. According to the minutes, he "earnestly admonished how [the listeners] should serve their God and Creator and be obedient, especially the listeners to their preachers, because they watch over their souls; also how we *should demonstrate a repentant life, and how grateful we should be that the good Lord still sends us ministers and messengers who proclaim and expound to us the Word of life and explain how a person should be constituted so that the seed which has been sown over him will bear fruit. It was strongly affirmed that all that we have heard in these days through His ministers and messengers is the fundamental Word of God, which will hold good and stand unto all eternity."*

Brother John's own minister at the time, the aforementioned Joseph Stuckey, was already in hot water with the more conservative ministers in Illinois—including Christian and Andrew Ropp, whom John mentions, and Christian Schlegel—for his lax enforcement of church discipline on matters of dress and his tolerance of eccentric interpretations of Scripture, among other things. Should we read his speech then as a defense of Stuckey, who had spoken on the first day of the meeting and did again immediately after Brother John?

Ah, we're getting rational and intelligent again, building great houses on the sandiest of foundations. We will hear more of Father Stuckey and the **Dienerversammlungen**. *But other voices are clamoring to be heard as well. Let us leave Uncle John there, basking in the afterglow of his admonition, a man of sixty-five but still hale and hearty, a solid citizen of what was no longer a wilderness, howling or otherwise, but well on its way to being an ordered and neo-European society, complete with congregations and meetinghouses and schisms.*

TWO

In the Land of Dreams:
Marie Gerber Strubhar, 1837

Well I never thought I would live in a house with no floor but dirt. No matter what you do to it dirt is dirt, and black and sticky it comes out in Illinois too, like nothing I had ever seen nor hope to again. When it rained the water would seem to rise up right out of the ground, and the bugs would all want to take shelter with us, and just keeping the mud off your shoes enough to walk was a task in itself, let alone trying to keep it out of the house. After the neat little places we had lived in Alsace, where no matter what else I had always kept the house clean and swept and the yard too, I'll tell you there were more days than one when I thought how crazy it was that I should end my life in a dirty, insect-ridden marshland, half the world away from the land of my birth. More than once over the years I made mention of who it was in the family had said all along that Jesus had never crossed an ocean and His children were not all called to either, and when they told me that this was the land of dreams I answered that I did not know who dreamed of dirt floors, enough mosquitoes to fry up for meat if we could stand to eat them, and wolves howling in the timber all night.

But even before my Peter died, back in the old country, I knew that the men would have their way in the end, and that if we were to keep the boys out of the army and still see them we would have to cross the water. So there was really not so much for me but to keep my back straight and my mouth mostly shut and let myself be taken off, across the ocean and over the land.

Such a great big world it is. I would never have believed it. We spent a lifetime on the boat, at least it seemed so, if not one and the

worst part of another. A hundred and thirty-one days and we counted every one, shut up in our tiny hole in the steerage, the five of us
in a box ten feet by five feet by three feet high, and a hundred others crammed just as tight or worse all around us. That's nearly two
months more than John had on his trip, which was long enough,
and why I don't know. Our preening fop of a French captain may
just have lost his way, for all the confidence he inspired in me. There
was no water, of course, but for drinking, and precious little of that,
unless we wanted to wash with the sea water and leave ourselves feeling dirtier than we began. And then the food. We had brought what
the letters from John and the others told us we should, as much as
we could carry: eggs, flour, potatoes, dried fruit, rice, noodles, sau-
sage, hams, onions, vinegar, sugar, coffee, tea, peas, beans . . . but for
all we brought, and all our stretching of it, we ran short with the
water still on all sides. Then it was going to the captain with our hats
in our hands, and for all his smiles and courtesies a harder man God
never let live, what he took from us for a few biscuits and a little
rancid butter. By the end it was one wormy biscuit a day and a cup
or two of water so foul we mixed vinegar with it just to stand it, and
the stench in that hold with all the sweating bodies and the filthy
toilets at either end—well, there's nothing to say now except that
all together it was enough to make me sure I was crossing for good.
Hell can freeze over, if you'll forgive me, before I go out on that water again.

And then we finally raise the land, praise be to God, and first we
must beat up the coast for two days because we've gone too far south,
and then wait for two more days in the harbor, and then stand for
more hours in the line to get in and try to answer questions in their
English, which none of us speaks nor has ever claimed to, before they
let us go on. A big city New York may be but it seemed to me not so
rich or wonderful as I'd heard tell, just bricks on the streets if they
weren't just plain dirt, not a one paved with gold that I ever saw.
There was horse dung and worse everywhere, and sharpers and scoun-
drels behind every lamppost, looking to steal the little you have. Even
then we were so far from our John and feeling at all settled, and from
what I've heard since we were precious lucky not to be robbed blind
and stuck in the city for the rest of our days.

But between Valentine and Lena and me we stuck it out and kept
a firm hold on young Peter too. I was glad to have Valentine with
us, even if he was only eighteen. We all knew well that in any country we knew of women far from home by themselves might as well
carry banners asking to be cheated, abused, or raped, if not carried

off into outright slavery. And Valentine learned along with us; we found that if he just acted strong and confident, even when he was just repeating what Lena and I had told him he should say, or what John had written out in a letter for him, usually things went all right.

From John's letters we knew to follow the same path he had taken before us: the canal boat to Buffalo, a coach for four awful days to Pittsburgh, and then another boat down the river for two days to Cincinnati, and a coach still half a day north to find him in Trenton. Such a country, so wild and empty, for miles and miles nothing but bush, the road, if you can call it that, just ruts and puddles enough to break your spine and leave your bottom bruised for life, and then out of nothing all at once a new town with log buildings and dogs running and men standing around spitting on the ground, laughing at each others' stories and then all at once pulling out their knives. They say the Indians are everywhere yet, but we saw not a one.

But at last there was my John, so strong and rough-looking now but still my own, I would know him anywhere. And we would have so much to tell, you would think, but after we all hugged and kissed and blessed God for finding us together again we stood there in the muddy street and just looked at each other for the longest time, not speaking a word. And I only cried a little and the boys hardly at all, and then John said, "Na, let's find a place to put your things and sit down." He had a little log cabin—just more than a shack really, but close to his work—and after the boat it seemed fine enough to breathe the open air, to sit flat with nothing to move under you and no need to hold your cup and plate or have them spill over everything.

Little Peter was so excited he scarcely took time to breathe. After we had eaten he wanted to see everything John had written about at once, the mill and the stable and the fields and the distillery and the storehouse with its jugs and barrels stacked up high. He was so restless that in a little while John said he would give him the tour, and Valentine and Magdalena said they'd go along too, but all of a sudden I was so tired, and though I knew the big water was miles and miles behind us I felt it under me again, never steady, always rolling around, like there is nothing to lean on and be sure of.

So I said I would just lie down for a little, and John my good boy jumped up and said he'd dust out the bed and fix it up for me but I said na, na, I would just loosen my shoes a bit and lay down on top of it, after what I'd seen on the boat a little more dirt, and of my own flesh and blood, would not kill me.

When I lay back and closed my eyes I could hear men shouting and horses clumping around somewhere, and I could feel the ticking of the mattress lumpy and scratchy right through the blankets. And I could hear some birds calling, not the birds I knew but loud rough sounds, Gaw, Gaw, like even the birds were saying this was not where we had been before. But for once I wasn't hot or cold or wet or hungry or thirsty, and no one's baby was wailing, and nothing was moving but a little breeze through the little window. And I blessed God again for bringing us safe to this new land and I asked Him to carry us on in the palm of His hand, and as I drifted away I began to feel that the great land under me and going out for so many miles every way, so empty of the people and the things I had known, so filled as it was with wild beasts and Indians and roughnecks and mud and bugs and disease and who knows what sort of dangers, was itself His great hand and would surely hold me up.

When John went to Illinois the first time, he told us more than once, he made it in twelve days each way walking cross-country, nearly fifty miles a day. But he was one young man walking with nothing but a knapsack. With a wagon and us women and young Peter, and in the spring with the water high and mud sure to be everywhere, he said we would like as not just sink into the muck and disappear entirely somewhere not even half through Indiana. They had been working some on the National Road, the newspapers said, and it was not even so bad in Ohio. But west of us (from all that we heard) it was still miserable on its best days, only what they called a corduroy road, with logs felled and laid sideways across it to keep a wagon out of the mud if you were lucky, rough and rutted enough to cripple you for life some places, and the rest of it a string of sinkholes that could swallow a pig or a child whole and not even belch.

So we paid the fare to take the steamboat from Cincinnati down to where the Ohio meets the Mississippi, thinking then to take a boat north up the Mississippi and another up the Illinois River to Peoria. Good travel we had that way at first, the water smoother than the corduroy by far and the boats slow but steady. We kept to ourselves mostly, for the people we saw were some of them so shifty and desperate looking we kept a tight hold on our goods and ourselves. One of them, a sharper who played cards and drank whiskey all one night, came right up to Magdalena the next day and asked her . . . well, I won't tell you what he asked her as I am a Christian, but John and Valentine stood right up and moved between them and soon enough convinced him that he should take his questions somewhere else.

So we found the place where the rivers join, and like a huge lake it looks there, the Ohio almost two miles wide and the Mississippi a mile. And we were put off at a little landing called Bird's Point to wait for a boat upriver as our boat chugged off downstream, bound for New Orleans where some of our brothers and sisters were even then coming in, the water route being so much faster and safer.

Ach, but we soon were wondering how safe we were. The place that called itself a hotel there was a house only, and with the roughest looking men you ever hope to see hanging around inside and out, drinking and swearing and bragging and carrying on. Two of them nearly made a fight with the hotel owner quarreling about who had paid too much and who not at all for the last night's lodging, and there was much loading of guns and waving them and firing them into the air even, with us over in the farthest corner we could find and trying to look like we weren't there at all. Finally they calmed down some, with no one killed or even wounded by some miracle, and next thing they were all drinking together like the oldest of friends. Some of the men eyed Magdalena again, but no one made any trouble, and finally on the second day a boat came upriver bound for St. Louis, and we praised God to be back on board and making our way again.

The Ohio had been a beauty to ride down, with its bluffs and hills alongside, and the bush so thick and tall coming down right to the banks in most places. When we started up the Mississippi, though, things seemed at once different, wilder yet and so still outside the noise of the steam engine that we started to imagine wild Indians behind every tree, even though John had been told they had all left Illinois except for a few far to the north. Dead trees and logs everywhere in the water, and swamps and marshes stretching off on both sides, so that it seemed the whole country must be half underwater. And then around a bend we come and there on a sandbar is a dead fish or something and two great birds with white heads look up at us and then hoist themselves up and go flapping away. Bald eagles they were surely, the symbol of our new country, though John told us he had heard it said back in Trenton that Ben Franklin thought the country's bird should be the wild turkey, which didn't eat carrion and was prettier besides.

Still, so strong and proud and beautiful they looked there, pushing into the air with their long wings, finding a current they could ride up over the river and away from the noise and smell of our boat, then floating above us calm and graceful, barely moving. Even if they were only gorging themself on some half-rotten fish and one of them carrying a piece away dripping in its claws, they were a wondrous sight. We all looked finally at each other, not saying anything but feeling how strange and grand it was to be there in the wild, riding a boat up a great long river to a new home none but John had ever seen, and that seven years ago. And I even had water in my eye a little, though all I could find to say was, "Na, birds there were in the old country too."

So three more days it was until we got to Peoria and unloaded everything and took the horses and cows and all slowly across the country to Rock Creek. By then some Amish families from Alsace that we knew at least a little had settled in already, the Farnis and the Ropps and some others, and we had written to them so they met us at the dock. A great comfort it was to know that in such a wilderness there were others of our kind that we could turn to for help and advice and gather with for worship on the Lord's Day.

Ach, but that was another day, that first time we drove up to the farm, seven years since John had been to buy it and longer since anyone had lifted a finger to keep it up. Getting there was itself a task, with nothing like a real road within three miles, so that Valentine said, "So, at least we have our choice of which mudholes we get stuck in." And crossing the creek was no easy job either with the wagon, and the water high from all the rains. But finally there it was amongst the big trees, the little house and the patch around it that had been cleared and the bigger patch of girdled trees too. Not quite all bush it was again, but close enough to bring us all near to despair, with saplings ten feet tall sprung up in the cleared land and the cabin roof nothing but holes and creepers all around the cabin and even inside, the well full of mud and leaves, and the split-rail fence all rotten and broken down. After the tidy farms, however small and poor, I'd lived on all my life, it seemed so ill-favored and haphazard that I could scarce believe it would yield enough to keep us alive, or that we wouldn't all go wild anyway from the sheer ugliness of the place.

Just at dark it was when we pulled up in front, and we sat there a long moment, all of us adding up how much was to be done just to make it fit to walk upon, let alone raise a crop or live like decent folk. Finally we looked inside, and with the mice and the rats and the squirrels and the spiders and the dirt floor and the trash and leaves scattered all over, it seemed even less clean than the outside. And I said, "Na, we can sleep under the wagon for one more night," which we did, and then the next day all of us set to cleaning and repairing and setting things straight, so that in five days we had at least a tight cabin with new mud chinked where the old had fallen and a good sound roof of fresh-cut clapboards held down by poles lashed to the purlins underneath. I swept pan after pan of trash out of the cabin, and dirt with it, until Lena laughed and told me I was going to sweep a basement under the place all by myself.

So it was sweaty work and lots of it for that whole summer, with land to be cleared so there would be something to eat that winter besides deer and rabbit and squirrel, and the fence to be rebuilt with mostly new rails and stakes and riders all around besides so that at least the cattle could not get in. In a few weeks Valentine and John, with Peter and Lena and me helping too, had the patch around the house that had once been cleared more or less cleaned out again. Only six or seven acres it was, but plenty when you must scrape every square foot with an axe or a hoe to root out young maples and oaks and weeds of every description from last fall, some of them tall as we were and tough as trees themselves almost.

The new growth was only starting, which helped a good deal, but still there we were from dawn to sundown day after day, with the sun beating on us or the rain pouring, chopping and hacking and dragging it all into piles to burn. The girdled trees from eight or ten years back were most of them still standing, but rotten now and risky even to brush up against—widowmakers, the people called them. More than once we would strike one on a backstroke or a blow that missed and some great limb would let go and crash down around us, and sometimes just a burst of wind would bring something down. Peter got a nasty lick on the head that way and lay abed two days before feeling up to coming outside again, for all that he was eager and excited more than any of us and always ready to work.

While Peter was laid up the flies nearly drove him crazy. I have never seen such a land for bugs of all sorts—when there had been rain and then two days of sun it seemed as though the whole earth and air were filled with them. Besides the houseflies there were sand flies, sweat bees, ants, ticks, cockroaches, all sorts of bugs and beetles who knows what they are, and of course the mosquitoes. Fearful hard it was to sleep those hot nights, with the cabin shutters open for what little breeze there was, the air so thick with water it seemed you could drink it, and then the buzzing and whining of the mosquitoes at every part of your body that wasn't covered up in something heavy.

You could bury yourself in blankets and sweat like a workhorse or throw off the blanket and think you would just put up with some loss of blood for the sake of a little air. But none of us ever learned to ignore ten or twenty or fifty mosquitoes all settled on and poking into you at the same time. A few hours of something like rest and then the sun would come up and the rooster would start in, and there was nothing for it but to get up and pour some water over your head and go to it again.

But I started to say about the flies: when Peter was sick one of us had to stay with him pretty well constant just to keep the flies from him. Trying to sleep he would be and they'd settle everywhere, on his face so thick that it looked darker than his hair in a moment. They got into the molasses and the honey and most of the other food until we got used to just spitting them onto the floor when we didn't see one in time. First thing after the corn was planted I set the men to splitting puncheons to make a wood floor, and that helped a good deal with not feeling quite so dirty all the time, but not all that much with the flies.

Still, I was determined that the place wouldn't be ugly forever. And indeed when the trees came out and the weeds came up it looked better—there were all sorts of wildflowers, names I didn't know, but some grew taller than my head. And I had brought with me right from Europe a few seeds and slips from my garden there, so that by the fall I had roses started and marigolds and larkspur in a little bed in front of the cabin with a stout fence to keep the hogs out of it. By the time we got our first callers, some folk from Kentucky who lived in the next cabin down the creek, at least I could feed them some bread and coffee and show them the flowers. We sat outside, on slabs the men had sawed smooth, with the sun going down through the dead trees and the corn and the weeds green and thick in the heavy air. A smoky fire kept the mosquitoes down, and we talked about our crops and our neighbors and the sad state of the roads, how we hoped to begin meeting for services every other Sunday and that they should come too if they liked. For a little while it almost felt like a place where a person could live.

There are no pictures of my four-times-great grandmother Marie, no character sketches, no biographical analyses. When she came to America in 1837 Goethe had been dead for only five years. Walt Whitman was working at odd jobs on Long Island. The revolutions American and French were long over, Napoleon had risen and fallen, and unrest and population pressures were driving huge numbers of German-speaking immigrants from the various small kingdoms we now think of as Germany. The official population of the United States was 12,866,020 in 1830 and 17,069,453 in 1840, the latter figure presumably including Marie and the rest of the Strubhars.

The United States of America extended as far west as the Louisiana Purchase, somewhere along the line of the Rockies in the north and more or less to Oklahoma (then the Indian Territory) and Louisiana in the south. What had been known as the Northwest—Ohio, Indiana, Michigan, Illinois, Wisconsin—was rapidly being surveyed, organized, and converted to farmland, despite the judgment of no less a man than James Madison, who wrote to Thomas Jefferson in 1786 that the "miserably poor" Illinois country "consists of extensive plains wh[ich] have not, from appearances & will not have a single bush on them, for ages. The districts, therefore, within wh[ich] these fall will never contain a sufficient number of Inhabitants to entitle them to membership in the confederacy."

By 1837 the center of population was somewhere in the middle of West Virginia and steadily moving westward. Ohio had been a state for thirty-four years, Illinois for nineteen. Martin Van Buren had just been elected president, by the votes of 765,483 of his fellow citizens, narrowly defeating the new Whig party, whose candidates William Henry Harrison, Hugh L. White, and Daniel Webster received 739,795 votes between them. Presumably neither total includes the vote of any of the Strubhars, who were not yet citizens (with the possible exception of John) and anyway, I suspect, too busy making a home for themselves to pay much attention to such worldly affairs.

And the earlier inhabitants? By the time the Strubhars arrived in Illinois, the mound builders who left their traces all over the state were long gone. The Algonquin tribes, the Michigamies and Kaskaskias and Peorias and Cahokias, fought bravely but not well enough in the wars for power and land that filled the eighteenth century. The Shawnees and Kickapoos spread into the open territory during the later eighteenth century and the early nineteenth, but in their turn were pushed across the Mississippi by white soldiers and settlers. The last organized resistance to white settlement was the Black Hawk War in northern Illinois in 1832, after which the surviving remnants of the Sauk, Winnebago, and Fox tribes were pushed into Iowa, and almost all of the dangerous humans east of the Mississippi were white. I cannot uncover any record of my ancestors even meeting a Native American in Illinois, though they must have wondered where they had gone. Even today my relatives turn up arrowheads in the deep prairie soil.

In 1840 Valentine Strubhar bought some land from his brother John, built his own house on it, and moved his mother and his younger brother Peter there. Marie Strubhar lived with Valentine and his family until she died in 1864. She was eighty-two years old, and by the end she lived in a house with full floors, plastered walls, good windows, and not nearly so many flies.

THREE

To the Black Woods:
Barbara Gundy, 1834

I didn't want to come at all. Certainly my life had been dull and poor enough before we set off for the boat, but when I thought of leaving it all for some huge and mysterious place, and very probably never coming back, I got knots in my stomach and spidery tingles all up and down my arms and legs. Though of course Father never asked me, nor any of the rest of us. We'd spent as far back as I could remember planning to leave, arranging, trying to get permission, even camping in the palace courtyard for weeks while Father tried to get some paper from the king. My little brother John was born there and loved to repeat the story ever after—"I was born in the courtyard of the King of Bavaria!" That was just one of the things he grew up to put on airs about, like calling himself John Von Gunden, as if he were of the landed gentry and not an Amish peasant like the rest of us. But that's his story, and this is mine, or as much mine as it can be, given that I did precious little but follow where I was told to go and work like a kitchen drudge or a beast of burden all the way.

When we left I was just fourteen. As I said we had always been pinched, with a cottage little more than a shack to live in and just a tiny plot of land we could call our own. Father tried to farm a little more land when he could get it, and worked out for the wealthier farmers at planting and harvest time, but it was usually potatoes and milk on the table for us, and there were plenty of times we could have done with more of both.

Anna and I did have some friends there in Darmstadt, though, especially two girls who were almost our age. Katrina was thirteen like me, and Hannah two years younger, born the same month as Anna. By the time we were leaving we had all just started to talk about which boy in the village might make a decent husband. But of course we knew that we could talk ourselves blue, or sigh and get sullen till we fell on the floor, and we wouldn't change a thing. Father was set on going to America, and he was the head of the house, and that was that. He had read the papers and pamphlets sent back from the New World, and the letters some of his friends sent back of the wondrous life to be had there, and he was convinced. Not that he was mean about it. He rarely spoke much, being so tired when he came back from working all day, and often gone for weeks at a time hired out to a farmer in another village. But sometimes he would sit me on his knee and read to me about the great free lands of America, how the soil was rich and there was so much land they just gave great patches of it away to anyone who wanted some, and how there everyone could worship as they pleased.

So that was settled, but just who would go was not so settled as we thought. Being so young, I never thought to notice that Mother was not well until just before Joseph was born. She was just Mother, cooking on the little stove in the cottage, soothing the little ones, sending Anna or me off for water or wood. I thought later what a trial I must have been to her those last months, with her carrying Joseph and feeling so poorly, so snappy and whiny I got when she tried to get me to help her. But a girl wants to be free, wants to play and run, not to chop wood and fetch water all day. And the girl I was then never really saw her mother, anyway. Certainly I never saw her as someone who could die.

When Joseph's time came Father sent us to stay with the Meisters, though I begged to stay—I was starting to wonder much about all this with babies being born. But we went, Anna and John and I, and as such things go we were playing around with Katrina and her brothers on the next day, laughing and running in the street in front of their cottage, when Father came to get us. We ran up to him, yelling, "Is it a girl? Is it a boy?" and then we saw the look on his face. "It's a boy," he said quietly, "and we named him Joseph. He is fine and strong. But your mother . . ."

So after that it was no more girlish games for me, not with John only four and always restless and all the work of cooking and washing and cleaning now left for Anna and me, but mostly me, and the new baby on top of it all. Father found a Lutheran woman in town who'd just lost her own child to be wet nurse for a little while, but she had others and could not spend much time with him. And before he was a year old the wet nurse was pregnant again and her milk stopped, and then he was all mine, all his smelly wrappings and his whining and his waking up all hours of the night and wanting the mother I could not be for him. Father loved his little boy, or tried his best to, but he was helpless with a baby and just made Joseph fuss more when he tried to dandle and soothe him.

So I suppose you could say that by the time we finally got word we could leave I was ready for any kind of change. Maybe, I thought, in America the food would be so rich and the people so kindly that I would get an hour to myself once a week or so. I even dreamed of going back to school, to learn more reading and writing. Of course it barely occurred to me that in America the people spoke English and what little German I could read and write would do me little good.

I did know enough to smile when I saw how the French clerk wrote our names down when we got on the boat—even upside down and in his scratchy hand I saw that he had "Jean Gundee" for Father and "Barbe" for me. But Father never learned to write so much as his own name in English, though his German hand was clear and strong. "God's language," he would say, "why it should not be good enough for the English I will never know." After we left the old country he never did care how people wrote his name down, though we teased him about all the odd twistings of it more than once. "A name is but a name," he said to me once, "your heart and your soul are what matters, and when you stand before St. Peter he will know how to spell them."

The trip to Havre far off on the English Channel was a hard one, trudging down the roads with all we owned in the world in the poor wagon drawn by our last horse, knowing that even by selling them we had barely the money to pay for our passage and a little over to start us off in America. It did make me wonder to see so many others on the road with us, and the closer we got the more of them, some with wagons heaped high with furniture and kettles and all else, some with nothing but their ragged selves to carry. "How could even America have room enough for all of us?" I whispered to Anna, but did not dare ask Father. Some others from our village, the Kiblers and the Meisters, were going with us, great large families both of them and the Kiblers much better off than we were with their new big wagon and their fine team, and so at least we had company on the way and enough of us together that the brigands stayed clear of us. When we weren't too tired we girls talked constantly about all that we'd heard of the new country and how we hoped there would be room and men there for us all together.

On the boat things were not so good either. The Kiblers had the money for deck passage and a cabin all to themselves, but we were crowded below in steerage, with the good Lord only knows how many poor souls like ourselves but smelling even worse. The food we could afford to bring was mostly potatoes and biscuits and dried peas, and we were afraid to eat that too fast and run short. The berths were crowded more than you'd think possible, a warren not even three feet high for the five of us to sleep in and a little share of the narrow hall between the cubbyholes for cooking and eating. Everything smelled when we got on and four times as bad after a week at sea, with the water closets always plugged up and too few for the women let alone for the men, who just went up on deck and did their business off the side of the boat. As Father said, it was just as well that we were hardly used to luxury. At least there was no wood to be chopped, and with only potatoes and bad water for days on end the washing up was not much. John found a pack of other boys to run with and was off with them constantly, getting into the little scrapes that boys will, and Father mostly sat with the men talking of where they'd go and what they'd do once they reached the new country. So Anna and I were left quite to ourselves for once, except for taking care of Joseph, and he slept a good deal once he got over throwing up. We'd find a hideaway on the deck in the hour each day we were let up above and let him stretch his legs while we dreamed our dreams of the beautiful houses we'd have someday, the servants to keep them for us, and the handsome husbands we would find.

Of course we had little notion of how we'd find them or what we'd do with them once we did. The few young men among the steerage folk seemed not even to notice me when I strolled around the deck with Anna and our friends, and I was not about to speak to any of the crew, the roughest lot I'd ever seen, with hardly a full set of fingers or a clear eye among them. One of them stopped me along the ship's rail one day, when Anna had gone below to use the water closet, and before I could so much as shriek he had his hands in places no one but me had touched since I was out of diapers. I yelled and struggled but nobody paid much attention; it was only Joseph kicking at his shins that distracted him for a moment. He backed off then, though I could tell by the look in his bleary black eyes that he thought I was a ruined girl—and why should I be bothered by his attentions? I didn't stop to explain, just grabbed Joseph and ran back below decks, grim and smelly though it was.

And I suppose that the boat was good preparation for being in the new country, though no matter how long you've been crowded, poor, and miserable you never get to taking much comfort in it. But it was a relief at least to be on the rivers and canals, where the waves were less and you could watch the scenery pass by, though all there was to see mostly was trees and more trees. I didn't pay much attention to all the times we hopped off one boat and waited to get onto the next, though we rode for two days on a lake so big it could have been the ocean almost, except that the waves were gentler. But mainly I just followed Father and tried to keep Joseph from falling overboard and hang onto my one little trunk and find a place to cook the little food we had left. And then we were met at the last boat by an old man Father said was Peter Schrock, an Amishman he knew who had already settled in Ohio, and he led us off down the wildest trail I'd ever seen, with swamps and darkness on every side, while he and Father and the other men talked through their beards all the way about land and crops and prices.

What they didn't talk about, at least not in my hearing, was the place they had for us there, to stay until we got on our feet. It was nothing but a log cabin, one not so big room with a dirt floor and a door and one tiny window that had to stay shuttered most of the time or the insects would eat you alive, which they did anyway. At that, it would have served our family well enough for a little; at least it was bigger than our berth on the boat and had a fireplace and chimney, and there was space outside for the children to play.

But of course the Kiblers and the Meisters had arrived with us too, and with nine Kiblers and fourteen Meisters added to the five Gundys I could see that our part of this grand new wide-open country would be not a little cramped for a while yet. The women put up sheets to divide off a space for each family, but with so many of us there was barely room to set a foot down without stepping on somebody's foot or child, and of course being the smallest family we got the shortest space. There was no question of getting beds for twenty-eight of us into the place; Father made a cradle for Joseph, but most of us just had to find a spot on the floor and curl up as we could. Ah, those nights in July, hot and sticky and still in the black woods, all of us poor souls sweating and turning and slapping mosquitoes, the babies crying, the young boys stumbling over each other trying to find the door, yelling like stuck pigs when they got stepped on . . .

One night after hours of all that I went outside at last, thinking I'd die without some air and half wishing that I would. At least the noises outside were just the little animals that were constantly about, searching for our scraps and leavings, poor as they were. I leaned against the cabin wall with my scratchy blanket over my head like a tent, hot and itchy from the insects and more tired than I'd ever imagined I could feel, and wondered what more could happen and how my life could ever be worse. I finally fell asleep that way, and though I ached in the morning from crooking my neck all night it was not much worse than usual. And the next day two more wagons drove up with two more families, thirteen more people, and you can guess where they were to be put up. When they started carrying their boxes and trunks into that tiny cabin already bursting with things and people, I wanted to run off into the woods and drown myself in some swamp. But I didn't.

After that I gave up entirely on sleeping in the cabin and Anna did too; we decided that if we were to be eaten it might as well be by the wolves and not by all the young men who were forever staring and using the crowding as a reason for rubbing up beside us. There were one or two I wouldn't have minded a little rubbing from, in the proper ways of course, Eli Meister and one of the new boys, a Binder from Alsace not so far from our home, but wouldn't you know that they were the ones that paid me no mind at all.

The settlement there in Wayne County seemed poor enough to me, though the people were prouder than any good Amish should be of it, with one brick store and their barns and fields and fences to keep the cows and sheep out of the corn. Most of them did have decent cabins, with wood floors and some furniture, and I had hopes that we could build one too and settle in and start to live like normal folk. But Father said we had not enough money for land here, and soon some of the others left to travel about and find a place for us. "Someplace where the sun shines," I told him, "without so many trees everywhere." He paid no attention to me, of course, me being only his daughter though I worked as hard as any grown woman in Ohio or the old country either. He spent his time mostly just sitting on a stump outside the cabin or roaming the woods while they were gone, though he did tend some to Joseph while Anna and I did the washing.

When the men came back they were footsore; they claimed to have walked four hundred and fifty miles, scouting out the land and then going a long ways south yet to register their claim. But they got Father all excited, too, and he told us to get ready for a great trip to our new home. "What's it like?" we demanded. "Is it all trees?" "Well," he said. "They say the soil is good, and the price is right. We will have much work to do, but I think we will prosper there."

That night I got Anna alone and asked her what she thought. "I don't know," she said, "it sounds awfully wild."

"I'll bet it's all swamp," I told her, "and mosquitoes big as sparrows, and wolves and panthers and bears ready to eat us alive."

"Well, what can we do?" she said. "Run away and live in the woods by ourselves? Marry the Kibler brothers?"

"We'll see," I said. "I don't intend to live my whole life in a cabin with one window and no floor."

So then it was packing and getting ready, loading everything in the wagon he'd made with the help of people in the settlement, and then we had prayers and sermons and singing and then off we marched, forty or more of us, after our Promised Land.

As far as the first town—Wooster, I heard someone call it—the trail was not so bad. There were stumps sticking up everywhere, of course, and mudholes to struggle through, but we kept moving. But the farther we went, the worse the way became, until the men and bigger boys were chopping trees left and right just to get the wagons through, and what was supposed to be a trail nearly disappeared altogether. For us girls and children it was not so hard as for the men, but it was dull and slow and the weather was hotter than I'd ever been in, the air so thick with moisture that it hardly seemed you could breathe it. Anna and John and I were panting like dogs on the wagon, and Joseph whined and complained so long that I finally gave him a smart lick on his bottom to quiet him down.

That settled him for a little, and then a great thunderstorm blew up and we huddled under the wagons and prayed not to die all at once in the lightning that was blasting down everywhere like God was half blind with anger and searching around for us in the gloom, and whole sheets of water pouring over us, no matter how close we huddled. There's another thing that was never so in the old country. It passed, after hours it seemed, and left us safe but even wetter than we were before, and not much cooler. We camped right there and somehow got a fire going to cook and dry out some of our things.

But by the fifth or sixth day of chopping through that endless forest I knew something was not right with Joseph. Only three he was, but already talking in great streaks and quick as a rabbit usually. But now he kept whining and said his head hurt. He wouldn't eat, and when I tried to give him water he gulped it down and then threw it right back up. I put a wet cloth on his forehead and went to tell Father, but he was chopping away at a big oak tree and just told me to dip a rag in some sugar water and let him suck at that.

Well, how can I tell this. It was two days more that we went on this way, with the axes always ringing against the trees and the heat on us like a great wet cloth. Joseph seemed to be a little better, at least he quit whining and sat quiet in the wagon hour after hour, and Father said that he was fine and would be even better when he saw our new home. But he barely watched the goings-on, not even looking around with his big round eyes but just staring at the boards between his feet. I felt somehow that he was slipping away from me, but I didn't know where, or whether he would come back.

Finally we reached a wide river that they called the Maumee. There was a little village there and something like a ford, but with the rains the river was high and the current strong, and before our wagon was a quarter across I knew we were in for trouble. Father slapped the reins and shouted to the oxen and they drove themselves forward, but the water came up in a swirl onto the side of the wagon, then over it, and the wheels came up off the bottom and then we were all thrown in. I kept a tight hold of Joseph, and Anna grabbed for John as he went over the side, and the river was not deep where we were. I went right down with Joseph until I was lying on the bottom with him, in the soft, slick mud—its smell still comes back to me today, sharp and greenish in a sickly, grasping kind of way, a smell of death and rot and things torn into bits by too much heat and too much water. My left hand went deep into the mud, over my wrist, as I tried to push my way back up. Finally I got my feet under me and pushed hard and broke the water, which came only up to my neck, and when I got Joseph's head up and wiped his face I saw him just looking back at me, not frightened, coughing and sputtering and tensed to cry or scream as I was myself. It was as though something in him had already given up, and he was just letting himself be carried along the rest of the way. I couldn't bear to look at him as we struggled back into the wagon.

He died four days later. After we finally got across the river, and with the help of the others retrieved as many of our things as we could, we followed the bank along to the southeast toward a place called Napoleon. The men had been told that it was a real town, with at least one mud street and a store or two, though we suspected half would be selling whiskey rather than honest food and supplies. I even had hopes of finding a real doctor there for Joseph, or someone who could help him at least.

But Joseph went no farther than a place called Providence, two or three miserable houses and a sign nailed to a tree. Six weeks on the ship, up and down rivers and lakes and canals into the middle of this huge dark country, two months in a cabin with forty other human beings, so good really all the time, eager to see the new sights and not complaining about the bad food or the cramped quarters any more than the rest of us, only to die here on a trail from nowhere to a one-cabin town with the name of a French tyrant whose head was worse swelled than these Yankees even. Ah Joseph, I remember when we got on the boat, those scurvy French sailors prodding us toward our miserable berths, and your pointing at the mast and asking where they got a tree so big and straight, to stand so tall and true.

You died in the night, Joseph, and I had fallen asleep beside you and did not even know when it happened. When I woke in the dawn, with the great trees all about, and just enough light to look into your little face and see that you were gone, I remembered your asking about the trees. And we put you into the ground, Joseph, under a tall, straight oak, and put a little wooden cross above it with your name on, though I have no hopes that it will last long. And we said a prayer for your soul, and I prayed for mine too and for all of ours, that God might know where to find us in such a great and cruel land.

So we went on to Napoleon. We found when we got there that the whole place was one cabin with one man named Hueston living in it, and him the dirtiest and crudest of all the backwoods rough-necks we'd seen so far. There was not even a track north from there and nothing to do but make one ourselves. The men and the older boys cut a way through the woods to our new place, which they came to call Lauber's Hill after Christian Lauber, who was with us, while the others of us tried to rest and collect ourselves, and to hear them talk it was quite an adventure they had, with their food running out and the mosquitoes in hordes around them, and their getting lost in the brush and then being welcomed to Lauber's Hill by another thunderstorm wild as the day of judgment. Father and some of the other men stayed behind to help keep the rest of us safe, for it was a wild sort of place, this Napoleon, nothing more than a clearing in the dark woods really, and more sounds and signs of big animals in the bush than anywhere yet. Father found bear tracks not half a mile from our camp, and one of the others claimed to have caught a glimpse of a panther. And of course nearly every night we could hear the wolves howl.

We went on then to Lauber's Hill and began the work of making cabins and clearing ground and all the rest. It was a dark and closed-in place, that season, with the heavy trees everywhere and the in-sects a curse and the rabbits and squirrels constantly raiding our stores. The Laubers got their cabin up first, then the Kiblers and the rest of us, though poor enough they were. Wood there was and in plenty, and water too—we had only to dig two feet down and wait an hour for it to fill. But the water was not so good as it was plentiful, and all of us had the fever one time or another.

The worst problem was food. We had arrived too near the end of the summer to plant anything, and before long the leaves began to turn and the nights got cool. It was good not to have the heat always with us, but soon our stores were all gone, and there was precious little to buy in Napoleon even if we'd had the money, and there was not even a gun in the settlement for hunting though the woods were full of animals. We ate corn dodger and mush until the cornmeal ran out, and then we searched the woods and the swamps for roots and berries and leaves for salad, and sometimes could make a stew that would fill us for a night at least. But with all the heavy work to clear brush and make fence we were soon lean and hungry as the children of Israel before God sent the manna to them. I even prayed that He would send us some, but never a particle did we find, only once in a while a muskrat or raccoon dead by the creek. We boiled them up and ate them in a flash, though they might have killed us just as quick.

It was around the middle of October when things came to a head. Father and Anna and John and I had been out splitting rails all morning, and when the sun got high Father sent us back to get the meal ready, saying he would soon come. Well of course he said nothing of what we were to fix, and as we well knew the cabin was as bare of anything to be eaten as the rails we'd been splitting. We were tired and hungry and light-headed from working all morning on water and mashed roots for breakfast. So when we got back and had set out the plates and cups we just wandered back outside the cabin and sat down to decide what to do next. The sun was out, leaning down into our little clearing, and with the puffs of white clouds it was a glorious day for us to starve in. We sat there, telling ourselves it was just for a moment, and of course then we drifted off to sleep.

We woke to Father's voice, as angry as I'd ever heard it. He went on for a while about how shiftless we were and how a man needed his dinner and how we must get up now and see to it. But we just sat there and let him talk, staring at him like we barely understood. And for all his anger he was too weak also to go on for long. When he stopped I spoke up to him, the first time I ever remember doing so. "We are all hungry, Father," I said, "and too tired to know where we might find our dinner or yours either. Where should we look for it? If you don't know, then we might as well die like Joseph, and let them lay us down too under some tree in this terrible black swamp."

I had started quiet, but I was waking up. "At least we could lie down and rest then, and forget the bugs and the fevers and the smoke and the work, work, work. It was not my dream to come here nor Anna's either, we have only been the workhorses for you to harness up and get to haul your dreams along for you. So let us be now. You'll find some other horses, stronger than we are, more able to pull your dreams along. Let us go to join Joseph and Mother. You can stay."

Father stared as though I'd struck him with the axe. And once I'd stopped I felt myself as though a great blow had been struck, and its echoes still humming through us all. I thought I should go to him and hold him, say I didn't mean it, take it all back and say I'd find us something, somewhere, for dinner, and we would be all right.

But I was too weak still to jump right up, and anyway I knew that I did mean it and that I didn't want to take it back. So I just sat quiet, leaned against the rough logs while the late birds twittered and jumped through the branches. And Father looked back and forth at us, solemn as a preacher, and then he sighed and sat down between us and leaned back against the cabin. He rubbed his eyes, and I could see then how thin and weary he was, too.

"Ah, my children," he said. "Did I ever think it would be this way? To work hard, that I expected, and to start with nothing, that I knew must be. But to slave away out here, twenty miles from a doctor or a store, with nothing to eat but weeds and muskrats, and the land so soggy that your bootprints fill behind you . . . This is not my dream, either."

"What can we do, then?" Anna asked, so quiet I barely heard her. There was a long silence before Father spoke again. When he did, I knew that he had been thinking what he was telling us for a long time.

"I have heard that south of us not too far, along the Miami River, is a place where our people have settled, many of them, and are prospering. They have mills and still-houses and big farms, they say, and a man can always find work among them, a place to sleep and food for his children. The land there is high, and we will have to rent a farm in the spring if I can find one. But if you can bear one more trip we will go there and leave this place to those who did not bury a child in it."

And so they left the black woods. By 1840 John Gundy, Barbara, Anna, and John the younger are to be found on the census rolls of Butler County in southwest Ohio, where the prosperous Amish Mennonite colony led by Christian Augspurger provided work and cash wages for many newcomers who were bound further west, including the Strubhar clan. The families may well have met there, but the Strubhars soon moved on to Illinois. In 1843, the Gundy family's tenth year in America, John married Mary Schwartzentruber Birckelbaw in Trenton, Ohio. She was a widow with four children, about twelve years younger than John, who was himself then about fifty-two. Despite their advancing years, Mary and John would have three more children together: Fanny, Jacob, and Jacobina, called Phoebe.

John Gundy and his family were not yet done with their rovings. In March 1851 John and his son John headed west. They traveled west on the Ohio and Mississippi Rivers to Keokuk, Iowa, Lee County, and after scouting around returned to bring back the rest of the family to Lee County. They became part of a great migration to Iowa in 1854–55, spurred mainly by cheap land: fifteen dollars an acre, versus forty dollars in Ohio.

Details of those days are foggy, at best. The Gundys seem to have been caught in some sort of land swindle, thinking they had clear title to land that was still under Indian ownership. But they remained in Iowa until John Sr. died, sometime between 1856 and August 1859, at between sixty-five and seventy years old. His son John Von Gunden remained in Iowa and became an Amish minister. Mary Schwartzentruber Birckelbaw Gundy moved to Illinois after John's death and settled in McLean County with most of her children, although the older Birckelbaws soon married and started their own families. Her son Chris began working on a farm for Rev. Michael Miller for eight dollars a month; he eventually married Miller's daughter. To complicate matters further for future family historians, Chris's sisters Elizabeth and Mary married two of Michael Miller's sons, and their half sister Fanny Gundy's first husband was another of Michael's sons.

And Barbara was also to end her days in Illinois. She married a Rudolf Eyer, had ten children, and died on December 15, 1893. It seems likely that she met and married him in Butler County, Ohio, and did not make the move to Iowa. One source says that Rudolf Eyer moved to McLean County, Illinois, in 1856, with his family. The record is silent on almost everything else about her life. She never returned to the old country. Very likely she was a farm wife. Her stepmother, Mary, may have moved to Illinois to be near her, but even that is guesswork. Was she prosperous or poor, sad or happy? She did not distinguish herself, nor did her husband, in any very large way. But her grave is in the Lantz Cemetery near Carlock, Illinois, much better marked than Joseph's.

FOUR ॐ

The Trials of Joseph Joder, 1872

I don't remember when I began to think that I was hearing far too much about hell. I don't know when the church I loved, God bless us all, had gotten so fixed on punishment and discipline that we had nearly forgotten the joy and peace of God. Perhaps it came to me midway through one of those nearly endless sermons by my good brother Jonathan, when he'd preached up from Genesis to the Prophets and was almost to Jesus, pausing to remind us for the fourth or fifth time of the disasters awaiting those who failed to keep good order and to obey the teachings of the church. There we sat, the plainest and most sober folk you'd ever want to see, churchgoers since infancy, hardly a worthwhile sin in the whole lot of us, and yet even my good brother felt he had to provide two admonitions for every word of praise. He wasn't the worst of them, either. I've heard preachers . . . but I don't want to name names or to speak ill of the dead or the living. There will be enough of that in this story. They were not the worst of men, and some of them did much good along the way. But they were men who expected to be obeyed, except for Brother Stuckey, and even he . . . ah, but that's a long story.

Always, over and over, there came the great warning, the great threat: that God had given over most of the world to the Devil, that all but His tiny remnant of the faithful, meaning us but not even all of us, would burn and not be consumed. It had never made much sense to me, that the great and loving God, the Creator and Father of the Universe, would people this world of His making with intelligent and feeling beings just so that most of them could be put under the most vile and hideous torments for eternity, forever and amen. I tried and tried to have it make sense, following the horses down the furrow, hooking and husking one ear of corn after another and throwing them into the wagon, feeding the stock, sitting through the sermons, but never could I manage it, not in English nor in German.

In the first place it did not seem to me a very kindly way for the God of Everlasting Mercy to have set it all up. In the second it just seemed not so very practical. Hell as I learned of it would have to be a very large place to hold all the sinners I have known personally, and as quiet and sheltered a life as I have lived. If you throw in centuries more of them all over the world, plus the Chinese and the East Indians and the Africans (who it seems to me can hardly be faulted for not knowing any better, but that is another quarrel), and all the ones to come, and if you think it is a place people keep entering but no one ever leaves . . . na. Even given no end of crowding and the great and infinite powers of the God who made the universe, we are talking a very large place, are we not? And constantly needing expansion too. Well this is all just reasoning and human pridefulness, I know, I heard it often enough, but still. Who gave me this head if he didn't want me to use it?

And all my reading did not help either. I learned Greek so I could read the New Testament for myself, and then Latin, and finally I even tried Hebrew though I never got so good at it, me over eighty already and trying to make those sticks and blots into something in my old head. But the more I learned and the more I studied God's Word the more it seemed to me that something in the way my people thought and talked about it all just was not right. It was like walking in White Oak Grove on a sunny day in springtime but only looking at last year's leaves and the fallen trees almost rotted back to soil, paying no attention to the new growth shooting out everywhere.

Of course I spent most of my time farming, as everyone else did. I was able to teach school off and on, but it would not pay enough to keep a family, and teaching letters and sums to children who would only come when their parents didn't need them at home was as much frustration as reward in any case. Now I have to say that many days farming I hardly had a thought at all; I was too tired from following the horses down the furrow all day to do more than struggle to keep them moving, to keep the plow in the ground, to make the rows as straight as I could, which I was never so good at as most of my neighbors but which did not seem to matter nearly so much at harvest as it did at planting time.

But there were days . . . especially those warm days after the deep winter and the raw winds and clouds of March, with everything blooming or budding out, when a man cannot help but notice just how beautiful the world is. On days like that, with the big clouds puffing along in the sky and their shadows sliding across the fields and the trees along the creek, with a dozen different kinds of birds noising around, with the first leaves coming out in a kind of green haze from the maples and elms and oaks, what man can look at all that and think of the God that made it and then imagine that God turning His beloved children over to the Prince of Darkness to roast on a fire?

You are wondering, no doubt, why we are listening to old Joseph brood about hell, when most of the current members of the church he belonged to live and breathe and worship out their days and hear scarcely a mention of the place. They would rebel en masse, I suspect, if faced with the kind of discipline that he lived through, not to mention the two-hour sermons, although we have it on good authority that even in his day the men and boys were given to wandering out into the churchyard for a little relief and conversation while the longer-winded preachers carried on, slipping back in just in time for the last hymn and the closing prayer. Although officially—so far as I know—hell has not been banished from good Christian doctrine, no respectable progressive Mennonite preacher these days would be caught dead preaching about it in any but the mildest and most tentative manner. It seems rather ungenerous by current lights, I suppose, to consign other people to eternal misery. And, we like to think good thoughts rather than bad ones.

So according to history, that untrustworthy judge, old Joseph may be on the side of the winners, though I suspect that he must find this posthumous triumph rather thin gruel. Still, I haven't been able to shake the figure of this tall, solid old man, walking behind his horses, brooding at his desk, prying Greek and Latin out of books in his spare time, driven by the eternal but not universal urge to understand the way things truly are, and to share that understanding with the others around him. In his own time, as we know, his thoughts were not so easily swallowed up in the gentle sea of tolerance that most of us swim in these days.

Old Joseph is still talking in my ear, in his slow, heavy, schoolmaster's English, telling me that he has just begun his story and that we will find it instructive at least, that we will learn things we should know about ourselves and our people. And since we are alive and breathing, for better or worse, at the end of the twentieth century, I ask you now to come with us, to put your questions aside for a little, to listen for a while.

So I kept my peace for years and years, even after we moved to Illinois, and a hard move that was too, living with the Christian Ropps for six months, trying to find a place to farm, and working like slaves to get started once we did. Twenty years I farmed there, with the debt from Pennsylvania hanging over me all the time, always too much work and not enough help. The daughters bless their souls did what they could and more, and Iddo too before he got married, but many were the times I wished for two or three more strong boys to work beside me and to mull over the great problems with while we husked corn or sat at table in the long winter evenings. Ah, we did well enough, and finally did pay off my old friend back East, and there were sympathetic hearts here in the West too, though not so many or so open as I had hoped to find.

That first summer with the Ropps I had some good talks with Christian's brother Moses, who lived close by. Just twenty or so he was then, but a true thinker who had read the Bible through four times already and knew it better than I did. Like me he had his doubts about what he heard preached on Sundays, but he was even less patient than I was in those days. His brother Andrew was bishop at Dillon Creek, and about the time we moved down to Rock Creek, 1854 it was, the two of them got into it. Moses was talking universal salvation to everyone who would listen and some who did not want to listen—in and out of the church—until finally the ministers decided they had to discipline him. So they had a meeting and were gathered all serious and solemn, ready to cast him out unless he repented and made public confession of his errors. The ban, we called it, and to be put under it meant that no church member could work or eat or so much as speak with you, even your wife and children; a grim thing it was for those whose families stayed in the church and cut them off short, and many could not bear it and gave in just to hear the voices of their loved ones again.

Young Moses was another story, though. I was not there that day but he told me later, and two of his friends who'd been waiting in the barn said it also, what he said afterwards when he came out to them, laughing almost: "Die alte Fohe, Die wille die Welt anzunden und wille die verbrennen." Well, that's strong talk and not bad German either, though it loses something in English: "Ah, the old fogies, they want to set the world on fire and burn it up."

So I wasn't alone in the world. But of course Moses and his family left the church after that, and I only saw him the odd time, once a year perhaps. And I did not want to leave myself, not once for all the way Moses did, with my brother Jonathan so much a part of it and all my other family too. Of course I knew people who weren't in the church, right up to Lincoln himself; he used to come into Versailles on the circuit court when we lived on the farm just west of there, and whom I spoke with more than once on the steps outside the courthouse. Not a handsome man, that one, and taller and more gangly than me even, but so quick, and ready with a joke, and yet with eyes that seemed to have no bottom to them, as though even then he knew he was meant for great and awful things.

And then there is Brother Joseph Stuckey. Yes, we have to talk of Brother Stuckey, do we not? He was one I had such hopes for, and to hear some of the people talk he ended up the hero of the age, the father of the church, and all because of what he did for me. Well, I do appreciate what Brother Joseph did for me, though still he could have done a little more. But it's a tale.

The poems had been appearing in my head for months or years before I ever wrote one down. Out I would be in the field, following the horses down the furrow or hoeing away in the hot sun, and mulling over some knotty problem of the Gospels like as not, when a line would start up in my head, and I'd hear it again and again and another behind it then, and another, until a whole great blot of them were ringing in my ears and I could scarce tell the corn from the sourdock. For a long time I put them aside, or tried to, and some I forgot or could not get to come out right on paper. But one day when I was in town I found myself laying in a stock of paper and ink and nibs, and then I was writing down the bits I could remember and then reading them back off the page, sometimes gloomy for how dumb and awkward they looked and sounded but sometimes thinking, well, not so bad.

When I had sold half the farm to Miriam, my daughter, and was renting out the rest I had more time, and then the poems just seemed some days to slip right out onto the page without me thinking at all. Now I am no Psalmist and I know it but they seemed to me not so terrible, and I even sent some to the *Pantagraph* and to young John Funk for his *Herald of Truth*. And did it not make me wonder when I saw my words in those pages, with all the smart folks? I was just a farmer and sometime schoolteacher that nobody had much taken seriously and never had asked me to preach or even to pray, though I thought always I could talk rings about some of our good pious brethren who spoke from the same verses every week and wouldn't know a real thought if it bit them in the lip.

Well and in the poems I could not help but find myself setting out all those ideas that I had squashed for so many Sundays, sitting on the benches with no backs. Not that I ever questioned God or Jesus or the loving mercy of His saving grace. But as I said, the poems did not seem my words at all, they just appeared under my pen, and then there they were. "The love of God makes all things well, / But man, for man, makes endless Hell." It still seems a good thought to me, and well put too, if you'll pardon my pridefulness.

So the brothers and sisters, or the ones that bothered to read, saw the poems in the papers, and more than you'd think sidled up to me after church or stopped by the farm to say they'd liked them. Even my brother Jonathan, as solid and respectable as they come, admitted they were not so badly done, though he also said they missed a big part of the Bible and I should beware of the bishops. The ministers were gathering by then every year or nearly, Amish churchmen from Iowa to Pennsylvania—except for the most dyed in the wool, who had already decided that except for their little flocks the church was all bound for perdition and past all chance of saving. *Dienerver-sammlungen* they called those gatherings, servant's meetings, though for all their talk of serving we were to find out just what sorts of orders they could deliver. Even without the strictest preachers there was still God's plenty of talk about *Ordnung* and *Gelassenheit,* ordinances and submission, and the need for discipline.

Jonathan, my brother, had helped to get the meetings started, and I myself went to what must have been the fourth or fifth one, just down the road a few miles at John Strubhar's farm, in 1866. Great numbers of the brethren came for the preaching (twelve hundred or more, someone said) and the first day there were people everywhere, inside and outside of the barn, far too many to sit down. Some ended up standing too far away to hear anything really, but they could at least talk about the crops and the weather and who was about to marry whom. I was still trying then to be a part of the whole thing and got there early to get a good seat inside and listen sharp, hoping to hear a true word somewhere. And indeed my friend Benjamin Eicher from Iowa, who of all those preachers was one I could talk to, one I still write about the weightiest things and know will not close his mind like you close the door of the cookstove, started things out well. He spoke of the need to listen to one another and to unite under God's grace and Jesus' blessed cleansing of our sins. He was out to visit again in the fall of '72 when it all came to a head, and he and Brother Joseph both ended up on the same side of the fence.

But I am getting ahead of myself. Next to speak was John K. Yoder of Wayne County, a sober man and pious who worked much with my brother Jonathan to bring these meetings about, and he spent most of the rest of the morning threatening the lazy and the apathetic, as though anybody who'd leave off in the fields after a hard week's work, clean up, put on his good clothes, and drive miles in a buggy or on a horse through the mud to spend the day on a hard bench or standing up just to hear a pompous old man tell him of his sinful nature should deserve to be called lazy. But so it went.

I had heard talk of a one-armed Amishman named Christian Erismann who had been teaching German school in various places round about, and between meetings I saw a man with his left sleeve tucked up and pinned. So as a fellow schoolteacher I went over and introduced myself and we talked school for a while. His German was good but his English poor, and when I hinted that the morning sermon had seemed a bit stuffy to me he acted surprised and said he'd felt greatly blessed and moved by the admonitions and exhortations. I had wanted to ask him what he thought about the doctrine of hell and such like, but just about then we were called back in for the afternoon preaching.

The next day, Monday, the real meeting started, and God's plenty of rules and regulations there were to be read and haggled over before anything worthwhile could begin. Brother Stuckey, being so bold, was a big part of the doings, and my friend Ben Eicher was one of the secretaries. Ben sent me a copy of the minutes later, all nicely printed up, and the regulations were full of good proper phrases, "Let us now be upright in love and grow in every way in Him who is the head, Christ, in whom the whole body is put together, and one member clings to the other, so that one assists the other, according to the work of each member in his measure, so that the body may grow in self-improvement..." and more of such stuff. "God is a God of Order," I heard them say, and I wanted right then to rise up and say, "Wait, now, I thought He was a God of Love." But I didn't, and they went right on with their rules, not to speak for more than twenty minutes at once, not to interrupt or mumble, but to rise and speak clearly and loudly.

To agree on all this took the whole morning, and then the afternoon started with more prayers and sermons, so it was nearly suppertime before we got to the first real business, which was to do with the Gridley Prairie congregation that had split the year before, with Henry Egly and Joseph Rediger taking off some of the people who wanted more heat and light in their services. They were having revivals and going around boasting of being saved and their sins being washed away; some of us thought they were full of *Hochmut* and vanity and an unhealthy interest in blood and suffering, but there it was anyway. Some of the pastors and Brother Stuckey with them went out to Gridley Prairie just after the meeting and thought they had smoothed things over a little, but there were bad feelings for years later between the two groups, living as they did in each other's laps. I cannot say it is true, but the story went around that on Sundays when they passed in their buggies on the way to church they would shout back and forth: "We have the true religion!" "No, we have the true religion!"

So the next days were filled with more of the same, with one after another rising to quote the Scriptures and proclaim his convictions, until I was full to bursting with their speeches and the little they knew being told at such length. They were solid plain folk, most of them, and had not read a book nor a paper save the Bible since their schooldays, and not learned much more than to read the simplest words and write their names then. Such a gathering of stuffy old farmers, like a great heap of straw after the threshing. I tried a few times to enlighten them on some points of the Scriptures and some of the Greek behind the German they seemed to think was the original language of Jesus, since I had just been studying it with young Miss Bottsford. But never did I gain any ground. I had even brought a poem or two, ones I thought were so simple and pious nobody could object, thinking that there might be a *freiwilliges* time for sharing. But there was never a time that seemed at all right. It was as I sat there stewing over it all that I started thinking: some way or another I had to try to open their minds to the whole gospel of grace and love.

The only one who seemed with me was a young reporter who'd stumbled on us somehow. He wrote up for his New York paper about this great gathering of backwards farm folk with queer ways and odd ideas about God, and how I had been the only one among the lot not ignorant as dirt. Somehow the story got back to us in Illinois and it did not help me out at all. *Hochmut,* I heard from all sides for a good year, is the Devil's work, and all that pride leads only to the fiery pit.

Still I did not just laugh and walk away like young Moses Ropp. I was older by far anyway, too old to just walk away, although many times I was tempted to tell the old fogies off as he had and make a clean break. But then I thought I could help someone perhaps by staying in the brotherhood, putting my thoughts in poems so that others could think about them without so much spiritual domination as we had always in the meetings, with the ministers in front all gray and grim. And when people would come to me and say, "Na, Brother Joseph, what about this salvation for everyone," how could I not talk to them? More than one went away having told me of years they had spent worried every night almost by the fear of being not good enough for heaven and a little easier for me telling him—and some of the ladies, too—that it was God's love they should count on and not His anger.

And then my dear brother Jonathan died, just in the first month of 1869. With him gone Brother Joseph Stuckey was the main preacher for us at Rock Creek, a good man and a strong man as I said, one I hoped I could talk with. When he first came to us from Ohio I had held myself back a good bit, trying to take his measure. He was a big man, nearly as tall as my six foot two and broader, gruff and solid, but his eyes could twinkle as well as glare, and from all the talk he was a man ready to listen at least to new ideas, a man wanting to stir things up right from the bottom of the kettle rather than let the stew stick and burn.

I could tell the first time we met, after services one Sunday, that Brother Stuckey had heard about me already, from Jonathan no doubt; he gave me that slow look that says, "Na, here is one to watch!" and held onto my hand for a long moment, not quite hard enough to hurt but almost, and got me square in the eyes with his own. "So you're the poet, then," he said, and I said only, "Na, some say so, but just a poor seeker like all of us." And then someone else came up to meet the new preacher and we moved apart, but clear it was to both of us that we would have more to do with each other, and soon.

And so I went on, writing a poem now and then, and a few turning up in the papers. When I wrote "Glad Tidings" I knew it was just what I had been trying to say all along, what I wanted so badly for my people to hear about God's love and forgiveness that it kept creeping into everything I wrote, even the one about White Oak Grove, which started out just to say what a beautiful place it is. But the glad tidings I knew had to be told somehow, no matter what the cost.

I wrote it first in English in the year Jonathan died, and a few people saw it. One of them was Andrew Ropp, the brother of Moses and Christian; he was bishop at Dillon Creek Meeting to the west of us. Now Moses was a freethinker, as I said, but Andrew was even more hook-and-eye strict than Christian and had never quite gotten over the way Moses just walked out on the meeting where they meant to excommunicate him. I always thought Brother Andrew blamed me for Moses' rebellion, although if he had ever asked me I would have told him that I never had to do any convincing with Moses, who by the time that I met him was already stuck in his views as wagon ruts baked in the August sun.

So one day Brother Andrew's wagon rattled up my lane. I asked him in of course and we sat down at the table and Miriam brought out some coffee and a pie she had baked the day before. He started out with small talk about how the corn was coming up and so forth, but plainly he had come with something more to say, and I knew he had been out to Archbold for the *Dienerversammlung.* And sure enough he worked his way around to the main point soon enough.

"Na, Brother Joder," he said, "have you heard what the ministers said about you last week?" No, I said, not a word. "Well I shouldn't say 'you,' should I, for no names were used. But it did happen out in Archbold that the question was raised, what should be done with those who insist there is no eternal punishment, but only in this life do men receive punishment, and all men will be saved. Now," he said, puffing up in my best table chair and leaning toward me, "how do you suppose, Brother Joder, the ministers answered?"

Now I could guess well enough what was coming. But it was one of those moments when you know you had just as well let someone have their say, because they will have it regardless, and the longer you put them off the more unpleasant they are sure to get, whether they have just eaten your cherry pie or not. So I listened to the speech he must have spent the whole trip home stewing over and memorizing, he had all the verses down so pat. And so I learned that such beliefs were unevangelical and that in Matthew we find this and in John we find that and furthermore in Philemon and suchlike.

"And the great danger," finally he concluded, wagging his finger at me, "is that the weak members of our body might be brought into this error, and their souls lost forever. And so it was that we agreed that any member speaking such doctrines should be set back from the meeting, broken up as the hard soil must be broken by the plow before the seeding, but with God's love and Jesus' grace and forgiveness of sins. And if they will not accept correction, they must be put under the ban, as true Christian order provides for, until they come to repentance and reform." And at last he stopped and looked at me hard, as though he expected me to fall down on my knees before him and beg to be broken and plowed up on the spot.

"Strong words, Brother Ropp," I said. "And who was it that put the question?"

His chin went down a few notches at that, and he spluttered into his beard for just a moment. "Well, it hardly matters who put the question, Brother Joder, when souls are at stake. You should know too of another question we decided, concerning what should be done with ministers who help to make rulings and then refuse to enforce them or to come to the meetings to explain themselves." He looked to see if I was ready to be broken yet. "And we found ourselves in agreement that such men should be visited diligently and interviewed with love, and if they will not enforce the rulings according to the Word of God, one must withdraw from them. So if you think that your Preacher Stuckey can keep you safe from the ban, you should think again."

Now I knew that Brother Joseph had been jumping into the hot water all over the place, helping the new congregations to the east at Weston and the north at Bureau Creek, near Tiskilwa. Brother Andrew had traveled to Bureau Creek as bishop for twenty years, but when Brother Joseph started to go up there many folk started to ask him to do their weddings and to preach, him being so much less strict and dour than Brother Andrew. And Andrew's brother Christian had been stewing because some of the Gridley Prairie people he had been ruling—well, serving he would say—as bishop, had just left and joined the Weston group. Brother Joseph had told me just the week before that it was mostly because the women wanted to wear hats to meetings and the men wanted to put brass rings on their bridles and such trivia, and partly just because it was too far to ride to Gridley Prairie from Weston, right about nine or ten miles for some families. But to Brother Christian such lapses were giant steps toward perdition, and he was having none of them. The year before, I heard from Christian Erismann, he had insisted right at the ceremony that a young man at Gridley Prairie take the part out of his hair before he could be married.

So it was then, with Brother Andrew staring at me over the empty plates and cups, and both of us thinking of the poems I had written, and of Brother Joseph so eager to push things along and the others just as eager to hold them back. And finally I said, "Well, Brother Ropp, surely there will be much to talk over after meeting on Sunday." I was thinking, of course, that a soft answer turns away wrath, and also that I would never get this stubborn old man to bend an inch and had just as well save my breath.

Brother Ropp hardly wanted to take such words for an answer, but finally he realized that I was not about to contend with him and left me in peace, muttering as he went about the need for discipline and *Ordnung* and for the elders not to corrupt the youth.

Ah, the tensions are growing, are they not? Though surely, as you know by now, the story is lacking in certain elements common to storytelling at the end of this century. I recognize the dearth of violence, sex, drug usage, or violations of legal codes. As a relativistic modern-day academic I have no strong personal objection to the literary treatment of such things, but old Joseph and the rest were not liberals on these matters. So the tale is mild and the stakes modest, as these people all were minor actors only among the Lincolns of their day. We are merely concerned with immortal souls won, lost, put under the ban, or held close in the bosom of the fellowship. The bone of contention is merely the true nature of the universe, the shape and substance of that world we see only through a glass darkly, and must either take or refuse to take on faith. The story is only about faith, and what it means to the lives of human beings to be full of it.

When next I saw Brother Stuckey, he had already heard all about the conference. And he was huffing and snorting plenty about the way it had gone. "Ach, those old men," he said, "they groan over mites and specks and care nothing for the real work. Parts in the hair and white aprons or black, when all over the country the people are yearning for the Word and for someone to encourage them." I said that there were times when I wondered if being in the conference was such a great thing that it was worth all the grief and aggravation, but he just looked at me sharp and said, "Na, Joseph, we must be patient."

And so patient we were, and he went on visiting all over the state, preaching and marrying and baptizing and giving advice and encouragement as he did so well, and everywhere the people either loved him or gathered behind his back to complain about him being too reckless and free with the *Ordnung*. And by the next Pentecost when the conference was to be at Gridley Prairie the ministers were so out of harmony with each other that no one knew what would happen at the meeting. At the same time, of course, they all wanted to keep up the good show and each appear more saintly than the one before. So what happened was the meeting went for two days with no questions, although there had been no less than eleven the year before. My friend Erismann was there and told me that Sunday was all preaching as always and nothing very strange, but the second day by the middle of the afternoon when there were still no questions handed in everybody started to murmur amongst themselves and more than usual slipped out to the privy and talked outside about the problems in the Illinois churches, which were mainly all between Brother Joseph and the Ropps one way or the other.

And the meeting went on, one admonition after another, until even Brother John Strubhar, the first Amishman to buy land in Illinois—a good man and a faithful bishop but one who almost never got up in public except to testify to the blessing of what someone else had just said—got his chance. And then Brother Joseph spoke, as he had on the second day, this time on John 10 and the new birth, and Erismann said he had them all in tears almost so beautifully he spoke, and some he talked to afterward said it was a shame a man like that could not have a little more concern for the old ways, and others said a man like that made them think that the old ways were not all so important.

Who knows who talked to whom overnight, but first thing the next morning, a Wednesday, the ministers all got together in the council room by themselves. Here there was no shortage of questions or of actions: they chose seven men to investigate things in Illinois, and those seven chose two Yoders, Abner from Iowa and Sam from Mifflin County, Pennsylvania, who were to find a third to help them do whatever they were to do.

Gridley Prairie is the old name for Waldo, the congregation I grew up in, and that afternoon John Von Gunden from Iowa preached—the son of John Gundy who brought my name across the water with him. John Von Gunden was half brother to Jacob Gundy, who married Magdalena Kinsinger, and Jacob and Lena had a son named George, who had a son named Gerdon, who had a son named Roger, who had a son named Jeff . . . among others.

John Von Gunden goes back to Iowa now, and out of our story. But I could not go on without giving him to you, my three-times-great half uncle, come from Iowa all the way to the plot of ground where stands the church in which I passed the humid and the icy Sundays and Wednesday nights of my youth. He spoke, I do not know how well, shortly after my four-times-great uncle John Strubhar at a gathering I never dreamed had taken place until a few years ago, when I read about it in a book not very many people will ever read. Should all this matter? What should it mean? Those are some of the questions.

So that was the '71 meeting, and Brother Erismann and I agreed it was marvelous how so much exhorting and admonishing about peace and brotherhood and *Gemeinschaft* could go on among such great and holy men while in the back rooms they were at each other like cats and dogs. In October the two Yoders and Moses B. Miller, another Pennsylvania man, came out to speak with Brother Joseph and Christian Ropp and the Gridley Prairie and Weston ministers.

So with them all in the same room once again all was peace and love and unity, or so Brother Joseph told me later, and they all said that yes they would work together. The report from the committee, though, was mostly about the ways that Brother Joseph and the Weston people should put themselves back under the old rules and regulations. It said that no church member could join another congregation without a membership letter from the one he was leaving, so that some of the Weston people would have to go back with hats in hand to Gridley Prairie and beg for their letters. And it said that everyone should stop wearing jewelry and "superfluous decorations" but be humble like Jesus, who I suppose never wore rings and brooches although as we know he didn't trouble himself about Mary, the sister of Martha, pouring out expensive perfume on him. And there was much about the Dordrecht Confession and Matthew 18:15, "If thy brother shall trespass against thee, go and tell him his fault," and on and on.

So after all this Brother Joseph was clear enough on just what the Pennsylvania brethren and the Ropps thought he should do. And he wanted himself to make peace, so much that he wrote a little book in 1871 with four of the letters from the Amish Division of 1693–1700, hoping as he said that seeing what happened in the past would help people see the consequences of division. Now what he really meant, it seemed to me after reading the letters, was that if some of his fellow preachers were to read them carefully, they would see the foolishness of being as pigheaded and stubborn over trifles as their brethren of two hundred years before, and creating yet another split among a people who were but a remnant of a remnant anyway. But of course even Brother Joseph would hardly say that straight out, in writing at least.

Meanwhile I had made up my mind to have my say, once for all, and to let the water splatter where it would. Mind you, I did not expect too much. By then I was beyond expecting and feeling more like Jesus going into the temple to clear out the moneychangers, though I knew the chances were good that I would be the one cleared in the end. I decided finally that I was an old man and anything they did to me I could stand, but that someone had to speak some truth and start some things to changing, so that perhaps at least the young ones could have it better.

I did not talk to Brother Joseph about it because I knew that as the minister he could hardly support me in what the rest had branded as the vilest error and danger to the weak. Still, I had spent as much time with the Bible as any of them and more with the Greek, and the more they preached hellfire and fear the more I was convinced that they were doing more damage than the message of joy and love and forgiveness could ever do. So I wrote over "Glad Tidings," in German this time, "Die Frohe Botschaft," with a Scripture verse for every line almost so that the ministers could not say at least that I did not have grounding in the Word for what I was saying. And I spent more than I could afford at the newspaper office getting copies made up. Then I had to find someone to carry them to the meeting in Lagrange County, Indiana, and to pass them out when the time seemed right. Well, I found someone, and such a good job he did that nobody ever knew who he was, and I am not about to give him away now after all this time. But my name was on the poem, though it was a hard enough moment when the time came to sign it, and so there was no hiding that.

The meeting that year was no easy time for Brother Joseph. First off on Monday afternoon, when they had heard enough admonitions to keep them for a little, they took up the report of the committee that had come out in October the year before. Right away various of the brethren rose to complain about its not being observed, which of course meant that Brother Joseph was not pushing the people hard enough not to wear jewelry and to humble themselves to get their membership letters from their old church before worshipping at the new one. So after much ado another committee was appointed, the first one on it Brother Joseph Burkey from Tremont, who was in thick with Andrew Ropp and already at odds with Brother Joseph about the church at Bureau Creek. The council went out and came back in to say that the problem was mainly between Christian Ropp and Brother Joseph, and that to settle it "Joseph Stuckey should be more patient, and should promise that, with the help of God, in the future he would exercise more care."

Now all this was happening with Brother Joseph nowhere in sight; he woke up with a sick headache that morning and was still in bed at his host's two miles away. So the first he heard of his promise to be more patient was when some of the others came back that night to tell him what had happened. You can imagine that the next day he was not exactly in a fair mood. In fact, after preaching the next morning, he went to John P. Schmitt from Gridley and told him that he would not have his admonition recorded in the minutes. Brother Schmitt, who wrote a good clean hand but was otherwise not so bold, put it in a footnote: "He asserted himself in these words: I do not want to have my name with something I do not know, and no one has the right to attach my name to something against my will. So it was done according to his wish and desire."

So this year there was no shortage of questions, nor of answers. There were groups having troubles between ministers and troubles about dress and troubles about the ban. And then near the end someone read my poem aloud, part of it anyway, and while I would not flatter myself I would say that at last the ministers found something they could agree on.

You need some of the poem here, don't you? I should warn you not to expect Whitman or even Longfellow; our friend Joseph was more concerned with getting his point across than with literary flourishes. His first English version is lost, but the German version with its regular rhyme and meter is more pleasing to the ear than the translation here, which is mainly mine, and my fault. Joseph wrote a poem to the effect that English was a clumsy and cramped tongue compared to German . . . But here it is, the best I can do. I have left out some parts and most of the Scripture references, including some verses about the Pharisees and how God loves even them and would not reject them forever and about the futility of justification by works. You can get the sense of it, I think, from what's here. It's not a great poem. And yet there is that moment at the end, envisioning the whole creation flooded with God's love, the earth become a heavenly kingdom of peace . . . I have read worse visions.

> The saying is sure
> And worthy of full acceptance,
> That Jesus Christ came into the world
> To save sinners.
> 1 Tim. 1:15.
>
> The teachings that we hear
> so often, of eternal Hell
> and torment, deny God's goodness
> and harden His spirit.
> Impossible. They cannot be true.
>
> We should mark the works
> of God the almighty,
> who does what he pleases,
> who creates and guides everything,
> maintains and governs
> and gloriously adorns this world.
>
> Even though we are sinners
> we are still God's children,

and all bound for glory.
With Jesus Christ our salvation
we are his heirs, his body, part of him,
brought back to God through him.

Sin itself must pass away,
God's grace and justice
only will remain.
The Redeemer, Jesus Christ
is the savior of us all
and will live so forever.

He teaches through our lives
and through God's revelation
that God is all-loving.
Must he not love his children,
even more than you love your own?

When pain comes to your child
it touches your heart,
you help him.
You don't give him a snake
when he yearns for fish,
or a stone when he needs bread.

God's love is far better
and his grace far greater
than yours, son of earth.
God gave us these bodies, made them live;
will he then give us
a scorpion for an egg?

He has promised salvation
and never broken his word,
and surely we believe him.
No hand can snatch
my inheritance from him,
or my security.

The gospel is glad tidings for us
because it brings peace.
Therefore the Lord of Heaven
sings loud and jubilant
to the glory of the Most High God.

· · · · · · · · · · · · · ·

Why will we not hear
the teaching of salvation
that God himself gives us?

Instead we sow the wind
and stay blind in the darkness,
deluded by our pride.

. . . .

Love flows out from God
and floods the whole of creation,
making everything into its likeness,
until the whole earth
shall become one paradise,
a heavenly kingdom of peace.

Well as I said I would not claim it to be the best poem and much
less in the English I suppose you must read it in. Still not the poem
but what it says seemed to me needful. And the ministers thought it
was important too, in their own way. They stepped all over each other's toes trying to be first to declare how much danger and heresy it
had in it and how pernicious for the young ones and all the rest.
John P. King being the moderator of course got the first chance, and
if you believe the minutes I saw later he spoke "very earnestly and
powerfully to the effect that this was heresy and wholly contrary to
the Word of God, and very detrimental to the youth, and it was distinctly noted that the godless person can comfort himself thereby
and calm his evil conscience." And it went on: "The attentive listeners were made very aware to be on guard against such beliefs and
heresies. An instructive remark was also made and clearly spoken
about the ten virgins." (Na, I know about the ten virgins, but who
knows what that means. I suppose it was clear and instructive at the
time.) "It was also distinctly observed that such church members who
have such a belief may not, if it is known, retain their membership
in the congregation."

There was a good deal more speechmaking after that, from what I
gather, mostly everyone lining up to say how firmly they agreed with
Brother King and how pernicious and dangerous and infernal they
thought the idea of a loving and forgiving God was. By the fourth
or fifth one I will wager you could almost see the haze of hellfire over
the dusty air of that big barn, and almost hear the crackling of the
flames in the rustling of the straw on the floor as the brothers shuf-
fled their feet and stood up to speak, and almost smell the sulfur
under the clean new hay, though of course it was just the dung from
the piles outside. And you would have thought that the dirt under
our feet was as thin as the first skin of ice on the watertrough of a
fall morning, and that if at any instant one of us uttered a wrong

word or thought a wrong thought it would crack and break for old Satan himself to rise up with a gleeful roar and drag us down to eternal torment.

The usual crowd of Easterners was especially enthusiastic over the part about not being a member. The Illinois ministers mostly stayed silent, though I would not take that to mean that they or anyone else there was much on my side. The proceedings go on to mention talk about "various letters which had a bearing on the above matters which had been suppressed," which means I suppose all the missives written by my friends the Ropp brothers and some others who had been looking for a way to get at me along with Brother Joseph for years. And then, the minutes say, the forenoon meeting was closed with singing, although whether they sang some grim reminder of the prospects of hell or a more cheerful song I do not know.

I thought Brother Joseph would take my side as far as he could, although I knew that he was far from believing the way I did. But even if he had wanted to speak for me, after what had happened in the days before there was not so much he could do either. And the afternoon was more stuffy admonishment about dress and about enforcing the rules: "the assistant chairman . . . made the point that these gatherings would be of little use to us if we make evangelical rulings if we do not enforce them and live them out and follow through with them."

The drift of all this was certainly clear enough. And I knew that when Brother Joseph came back we would have some high words about the poem and my sending it to the meeting, although I did not know of all the other grief Brother Joseph would find there and how harassed and pressured from all sides he would feel by the time he got on the train to come home. But the next Sunday he came to services with my poem in his hands, and afterwards he strode up to me and asked if it was my doing. "Well my name is on it, Brother Stuckey," I said, "that's plain enough." "Well," said Brother Joseph, "you can't be a member."

So it was said then and no turning back. And yet that was not the end, not nearly, and it was in the next weeks and months that Brother Joseph and I became closer than ever in our ways, without ever managing to agree. For though he told me flat that Sunday that I could not be a member without taking back what I had said, still Brother Joseph had no will to turn me out just like that. Instead we talked, ach, how we talked, starting that very afternoon when he insisted Miriam and I come home for dinner with him. When the plates were cleared away he told me the whole story of the meeting, sparing nothing and no one. I was with him in his struggles with the Ropps and the hook-and-eye nitpickers and he knew it, and that did not make it easier for him when we got to the poem.

"Na, Brother Joseph," he said, with a long square look of the sort I used on pupils who were smart but too noisy and shifty for their own good, "think of what you're saying. Of course there's too much hellfire preaching and talk of the torments of damnation. But where are we if we let that go altogether? If we say that everyone will be saved, what reason is there not to do whatever we will, to be drunken and idolatrous and worse? Why should the young pay us any mind at all, if in the end they'll get their wings and harps whatever they do?"

I had thought about that myself. "Is there nothing within us then but evil? Must we be frightened into obedience? Will not God's spirit and the grace of Jesus move us, speak to us, without pitchforks and flames to prod us? Should we not preach the good news for what it means here and now as well as in the next world, that the joys of living in Christ are greater than the pleasures of the flesh? And will our hearts not be moved by the glad tidings if we are truly meant to hear them?"

Well that started us. And on and on we went, all that afternoon and over supper too, with the women looking in from time to time and shaking their heads and pursing their lips and then leaving us to our disputation. It wasn't to be won or lost that day, or in the next days, though every time we met we somehow found ourselves going over that same ground again.

Still Brother Joseph did not set me back from the church. When I asked him at the end of one long argument why he did not just ban me and have done with it all, he first laughed and said, "Na, why not?" And then he went serious, and he said, "Ach, I have seen too often, Joseph, that the one cast out becomes like a branch cut off, that withered and was lost, gone from the fellowship for good. Too many have gone bitter and faithless and not repented but become more stubborn and stuck in their ways. And also," here he got that glint in his eyes again, "dear Joseph, if I cast you out for the heretic that you are, who will there be to argue with me so long and close?"

So it went on until the fall, though in the meantime we were all caught up in our usual lives of course. That was the year that we were building the new meetinghouse, and Brother Joseph asked me to write the dedication hymn, which I did, though he told me plain enough he would have no universalism in it. Just for him I made it as sound and orthodox as I could, although there's no hell in it either, but much of the joy and gladness of living in Christ's blessing.

But the Ropps and some of the other bishops had been waiting to see what Brother Joseph would do, and when they found that not only had he not excommunicated me but had given me the dedication hymn to write they were higher on their horses than ever. They got three ministers from the East to come out and put their noses into every corner and see what to do. They came on the train into Chenoa, where Preacher Christian Schlegel from Gridley Prairie met them, and you can be sure they had two or three earfuls by the time the horses got to his place even if it was three in the morning. So they preached and had meetings around the area for a week and more, and Brother Joseph and my friend the Reverend Ben Eicher who'd come from Iowa for the church dedication went twice to be with them. Finally on the tenth of October they came to North Danvers and the new meetinghouse, and Christian Ropp and Christian Schlegel and brethren and sisters from all over the state were there for the big service, including me of course, although much of that crowd refused to greet me but looked slant-eyed at me all through the meeting. Afterward the three from the East took Brother Joseph off into the back room, and when they came out he was looking grim and thunderous enough and they also. But there was still visiting to do, and such a great crowd of neighbors and such that I could not get close to him and finally decided to get on home myself.

I was on the drive home, letting my horse find the road and brooding on all that had happened, when I saw a wagon behind a little stand of trees and recognized it for Brother Joseph's. He pulled out beside me as I came up and we rode along together in silence for a while as the horses clopped along. I looked over and he had that stony look again, like some prophet who was just biding his time. Finally he looked at me. "Well, Joseph," he said, "it's in the fire now. They asked me did I still consider you my brother, and for all the time we've spent wrangling and arguing I still did not know what I would say. But like the fool I am, when that was the question I said, 'Ja, I hold him as my brother, and have gone to communion with him.' And so they did not ask me if I believed your universalist foolishness or any of the rest of it; they just went all silent and hard and said I should go, and they would make their report."

The horses clopped along the road for a little. "Thank you for sticking to me, Joseph," I said, "though what will come of it I don't know, with that tribe of stiff old men thinking they rule the world. Will there be a church someday where we can come together in good faith

and argue and dispute and pray together without some of us thinking they have to rule all the rest?"

He did not answer. We rode along for a while, chewing on it, and
then we turned west and rode on where the sun was going down in
front of us, so bright and low that we could barely see what was coming, and only had to trust in God that nothing too awful was.

*And so we leave old Joseph and Father Stuckey, as they make their way
home. The committee withdrew from Stuckey "in the matters of fellowship and the holy kiss," but Stuckey's church supported him, and so did
the others at Weston and Washington. He traveled almost constantly for
the next twenty years, helping to start new congregations and support others, and a group formed known as the "Stuckey Amish." After over twenty
years with no official organization, held together almost entirely by the
force of his personality, twelve congregations formed the Central Illinois
Conference of Mennonites in 1908. By 1926 there were twenty-six churches.*

*The year after Stuckey was put out of the conference, under pressure from
members of his own congregation, he told Joseph Joder that he could not
take communion until he changed his views on universal salvation. Joder's
response was to stop attending church altogether. He lived out his life in
bookish retirement, studying the Bible, writing letters to his friend Ben Eicher, whose church in Iowa also left the Amish conference. In the winter of
1879, at the age of eighty-two, Joder began to study Hebrew with the aid
of a young woman who had recently graduated from Illinois Normal University nearby. According to his grandson and biographer Olynthus Clark,
in his old age he would periodically vow to quit smoking, and throw the
pipe he had used all of his life as far away as he could. But he always
managed to find it again. One quatrain written in his last years survives,
from a letter to Ben Eicher:*

> My sight is dim, my hearing dull,
> My eyes are eighty-seven, full,
> I am waiting for the Master's call,
> May God have mercy on us all.

*He died in 1887, in his ninetieth year, and is buried in the Lantz Ceme-
tery near Carlock, Illinois. His headstone is placed at a right angle to all
the rest.*

FIVE

From Waterloo to New Orleans: Peter Nafziger, 1882

Other people's business, that's what she'd call it. And I'd say it was the Lord's business, after all, and then she'd say that some of the brethren seemed to manage without my traipsing all over the country to minister to their needs and she was hard put to see that the rest could not get by without me also, especially those folk way off in New Orleans, two weeks' walk each way if I didn't get distracted by some hive of barefoot backwoods shanty dwellers and spend another week eating their venison and bear and serving them communion with only wild turkey breast for bread and corn whiskey for wine. Now, Barbara, that only happened the one time, I would say, and it was only three days. And it only made four and a half weeks you were gone, she'd say, and the very heart of harvest season, and the boys and I left to pick every shabby ear of corn that managed to outlast the butterprint and lamb's-quarter because you were off gallivanting in Pennsylvania when you should have been cultivating.

Over the years I tried various ways of answering my Barbie when she got onto the subject of my unsatisfactory overall performance as farmer, husband, and provider. I tried reason and churchly piety and quoting Jesus (all that got me was "You're not Him") and claiming my authority as head of the household ("You're more the body than the head, running across the country like a headless chicken"). I tried getting angry, getting quiet and polite, not saying anything, going out to the fields and working. Overall, none of it worked, mainly because considered in most lights she was right, and we both knew it. I was never such great shakes as a provider, always too restless to put myself to farming week in and week out, too easily caught up in what was happening in the next county or the next state or anywhere beyond the boundaries of whatever little patch of ground I was supposed to be pouring all my sweat and concentration into.

Even when I first wanted to leave Hesse and come across the water I had the Devil's own time to persuade her to leave. "Our home is here," she would say in that stout way of hers, and all of my talk of the great opportunities for ministry and of the marvelous open lands in Canada might as well have been addressed to the door as to Barbara's ears. She would have been content forever on the Gieser Hoff, our little farm, fair crops or none, and all that convinced her to come along was the idea that in Canada there were no landlords or kings to press a sword into our sons' hands and send them off to die for some nobleman's honor.

So when finally all was settled and we made the great journey, we found that Canada was good land and pretty, yes—but ach, it was cold! The old country was nothing like it even, winters that lasted half the year long, snow up to the horse's belly, the creeks and even the rivers frozen solid, just getting water to keep the stock alive a full day's work sometimes. And dark until noon almost and then dark again before suppertime, and all of us huddled in the cabin trying to keep one side at least unfrozen at the fire.

So we were there five years, and the brothers and sisters in Ontario were good, but then I went down to Cincinnati and stayed with the Augspurgers for a few weeks, visiting and preaching and doing some church business. And I saw how beautiful the land was there by the Big Miami River, the hills and all, and how well they had it, with big stone houses and mills and distilleries such as I'd never seen. It seemed a place where the poorest man could get rich—now I know what the Good Book says about laying up treasures here below, mind you, but I never did hear that the Savior said a man should turn aside from honest labor and its rewards. And my talents were so little for laying up that I never much had to resist that temptation.

I did have some talking to do once again to get Barbara and the family willing to make the trek to Ohio, that's for certain. Myself I've never minded the traveling if there's something worth finding at the end. Ach—I might as well admit it—I love to be out on the road even if I don't know what's at the end. So they weren't keen at all at first, but about the middle of February, with four or five feet of snow outside and the wind yowling around the cabin worse than the wolves and the stew left from supper frozen in the pot, well, they started to see my way of it.

And I told them what I had written to my friends in Germany, that the wages for a day's work were a full half a dollar and the fields of wheat and clover more beautiful in the spring than any I had seen since leaving the old country, and the distilleries all ready to make whiskey that sells for fifty cents the gallon quicker than you can turn it out. Yes, if we'd known all this we'd not have come to the North to start. But truly we must trust that it was God's will, and the brethren we left behind in Ontario surely were a blessing to us, and we to them in our small way also, let us hope.

And so we gathered up the children and the household goods and found forty acres to buy near Trenton, in Milford Township, where Christian had just built his great new stone house and called it Chrisholm, like some manor house. But then he had been accustomed to living high. He had managed the farm of some big spy for Napoleon before coming over and now was making money hand over fist from the whiskey and hardly able to give it all to the church, so who could blame him? A pious man and sober himself he was, but with such a knack for finding the way forward in the world. It's not my place to speak ill of the man. And no one can deny that more good work was done with the money he made selling whiskey than if he'd mired a hundred wagons in the muck hauling corn in sacks to Cincinnati.

We were barely settled in Ohio when Johannes Engel and Johannes Weyrey stopped by to stay with us and take a rest from their own journeying. They had been to Illinois and were all starry in the eyes just talking about it—the Promised Land, they kept saying, it is the Promised Land. We know these great prairies now, but I had never then heard of such a thing, like being on a ship in the sea, they said, and the grass taller than a man (at least a short man like you, Peter, said Engel, and laughed) some places and thick everywhere, and plenty of timber and creeks full of fish. Engel was bound to New Orleans to meet his father and sisters and some other friends and said they would go up the Mississippi to the Mackinaw or the Illinois or the Rock River and get land and start a new church, and so they did, though all the details I didn't hear until years later.

But the land in Ohio was good enough for us then and our health was too, so I praised God and began to work to cultivate what was set before me. I found plenty to do both on the farm and with the church there, though we soon knew we'd come too late to get rich like the Augspurgers, not having their whiskey business and their grist and lumber mills and their farms on top of farms. It was really the church that I cared for most anyway, or so I told myself and believed it, too, most of the time. The old Bishop Krehbiel was ready to retire, so it was Brother Jacob Augspurger and me for bishops, and then Peter Schrock was a minister too, and with Sunday service and weddings and funerals and all we kept busy.

Still we kept hearing from the other brethren, so many then were scattered far to the west and in the south, a few here, a few there, some of them giving in to the world already. I made a trip to Illinois to preach a little and to marry a young couple or two and to see the place for myself—it was rich and beautiful of course, though after a few hot summer nights with the mosquitoes on me like fur I began to think that the tellers of all those stories I'd heard had not spent July in the place. Then I heard of some folk in Kentucky that wanted a minister and so went to them for a few weeks but had to come back for the harvest.

I sometimes took a horse for the trips, and everywhere I went the people were friendly with a night's stay in the barn and a meal and eager to hear the Word, so that I took joy in the fellowship and tried to leave everyone heartened. But most often I would walk if I could—the going was slower but there's nothing like a fine day in the outdoors and just a little sack on your back and a staff to hold in your hand, going ahead down a path that perhaps not twenty white men have ever walked, not knowing where you'll lay your head that night.

People say now what a boon the new roads are—laid out straight as strings along the section lines, some of them even paved with crushed rock and passable in a wagon even in the worst weather. I have to say, though, that I miss those old wavering tracks, for all their stumps and sloughs and mudholes that could drown a man and swallow a boy in a gulp. How many times did I walk the better part of a day down one of those paths without seeing another human face, with the insects in clouds around me and the mud up to my knees? Then if I was lucky toward the end of daylight I would spy some broken-down hovel and a woman inside kneading dough on an oilcloth not much cleaner than the slough. And I'd kindly ask her for traveling mercies and perhaps sit with her children while the supper was cooking and tell them about the straight and narrow way that leads to salvation, thinking in my mind that if they'd a steady diet of her bread, and the dirt and ash she was mixing in with every turn of it, they might be in need of salvation soon enough.

So much I saw, so many people, some of them rough as corncobs and far from your sober Christians, surely, but all in all they were ready to help a man when they found he was traveling on the Lord's work, and when I talked of the grace of Jesus to them not so many turned away. Even in the wicked city of New Orleans there were good folk to be found amongst all the temptations and the fleshpots, and besides preaching and exhorting the brethren to stay on the goodly path I was also able to tell them of the fine land to be found up north and that they should linger in the city no longer than they had to. And a good many came then, to Ohio and later to Illinois, and who is to say if they might have fallen by the wayside and been trampled under foot if not for my small presence among them.

Things in Ohio, though, had begun to go a little sour. A good many of my Hessian brothers and sisters began to come to Butler County in the years after we came, and before you knew it there was trouble. The Augspurger crowd were Swiss Amish and hook-and-eye believers, good people but strict-seeming, and not a little stuck on themselves too some thought, and all their fine houses and mills did not make them any more humble certainly. They had no quarrel with earning good coin, the Lord knows, but they couldn't abide the buttons and the mustaches and the dancing that the Hessians brought along, much less the piano. They were sure it was worldliness and sin and the Devil himself hiding in each fancy button and lurking inside the polished wood of the piano box, weaving snares to pull good Christians down to hell.

Well now I wouldn't judge myself, you understand, but they made up their minds in those first months, once and for all it seemed, and it grieved us all but soon we knew that something had to happen. One wet spring, 1835 it must have been, we met and prayed together and decided the first group should meet in one place and the Hessians in another. I had no special quarrel with either of them, but went to minister to the Hessians, since I was from there myself and they needed a preacher. The other Amish soon built a church house, but we met in homes for as long as I lived there in the old fashion. We had less money, of course, but some of the brethren were not above mentioning who was being faithful to the old ways in this regard. I suppose God can settle all that up in His own good time.

But not long after we started to think again about moving on. Young John Strubhar, who worked for the Augspurgers, had gone out and bought land in Illinois already in 1830. He kept talking of how he would go live there and get rich once he got the money to bring his family over from France. Two men's work he did for two solid years, that John, saving up every penny, and then just when he'd sent the money he got word that his father had died, skinning some muskrat or squirrel and got the blood fever. But his mother and brothers and half sister did come then, and sure enough before long they were gone to Illinois where they did very well, thank you.

In my family it was the other preachers who were to make the move first, though—Michael Kistler who married my daughter Elizabeth went already in '41, and my Magdalena and her husband the Reverend Michael Kinsinger even before. It was 1844 before we decided to follow them, when I was fifty-five years old and, Barbara said, getting old to be starting all over, though I still found myself hale and hearty through God's grace. So we found a farm near Congerville and stayed there, and I was able to keep on the go and help the brothers and sisters all the way down in New Orleans and up by Tiskilwa too.

When Peter came over in 1826, the part of central Illinois where he lived out the last forty years of his long life was still mostly virgin prairie, with scattered homesteads in the timbered areas and a few tiny towns along the rivers. By 1885, when he died, the prairies were opened and settled, and the farm population of Illinois may have been higher than it is today, given that a hundred sixty acres with some livestock could support a family of ten and a hired man. The roads had improved greatly, with straight roads laid out beginning in the middle of the century on the mile-square grids imposed by the Land Ordinance of 1785, and the more traveled ones already improved with gravel or even paved. With the woodlands disappearing, some enterprising farmers began to plant hedgerows of osage orange, locust, barberry. In Illinois these would also disappear, along with most of the fences, with the rise in land prices and decrease in pasturing of cattle during the 1960s and 1970s. I remember the hedgerow that ran west from my parents' place and the great pile of twisted, fractured branches and orangish roots that the man with the Caterpillar left for us to burn after he'd tractored it out.

The philosophy and legalities of fencing also shifted. No longer were there enclosed fields surrounded by free lands for grazing—long before the end of the nineteenth century, a pasture in Illinois was a private field with a fence around it to keep the animals in, not out. This privatizing was hard on the poorest farmers, who relied on common lands, but helped keep the cattle and hogs of less finicky citizens out of the gardens and flowerbeds of the rest. Now lawns could stretch uninterrupted from the house to the road, although on my home place the front yard was fenced in until the sixties, when we built a new house next to the old one. The cheap and portable fencing allowed by barbed wire also encouraged the use of heavy machinery, allowing easy access to fields and shifting of boundaries.

But what did the country look like? The descriptions vary wildly. Some travelers complained of the monotony of the landscape, saying it was all the same from Pittsburgh to the Missouri River. According to J. B. Jack-

son, *"Writing in 1850, an English traveler described the American land-scape as 'ugly and formal'—ugly in its stumps and dead trees, in the lit-ter-strewn yards, the waste everywhere in evidence; formal in its long straight roads or roadways, its large rectangular fields, its bleak, rectan-gular little houses, its hilltop churches painted a blinding white, its clas-sical placenames."*

On another hand, here's Eliza Farnham in 1846: "Spring morning on the prairies! I wish I could find language that would convey to the mind of the reader an adequate idea of the deep joy which the soul drinks in from every feature of this wonderful scene! If he could have stood where I have stood . . . he would feel one of the charms which bind the hearts of the sons and daughters of this land."

There's much more, about the vast majesty of the prairies, the heavy dews, the friendly presence of the trees, the grouse and robins and whippoorwills. One moment she's musing on "how many ages that plain had been spread out beneath those soft skies and that genial sun; how its flowers had bloomed and faded, its grasses grown and decayed; how storms had swept over all its wide expanse, and the thunder echoed from its bosom; how the solemn winds of autumn had sighed over it, and the raging fires marched in unre-strained fury from one border to the other; how long all this power and mag-nificence had displayed itself unseen of any eye, save His who made it!" and the next she's imagining "files of dark warriors stealing silently along, unmindful of the flowers and the bright skies, . . . intent only upon the fierce butchery to which they were marching."

As we'll all note, Farnham seems to have absorbed, not unusually for her time, a rather limited image of the Native American . . . but let it go, let it go. In other passages her Illinois is parched by drought, battered by storms, aswarm with mosquitoes, and aswim in mud. Was this Illinois then a moderate land of beauteous wildflowers and gentle rains? A howl-ing place of tornadoes and thunderstorms, prairie fires and blizzards? A swamp or a desert? An empty room waiting for white men and women to fill it or a full house unable to defend itself against marauders from the East? Even given the slow travel of those days, many of the reporters were, essentially, tourists. Eliza Farnham stayed three years in Illinois, not as long as my ancestors, but long enough to know that the answer to all of these questions is yes.

In those years it was that the young men began to come and tell me God was pointing them toward some man's daughter and would I please drop by and ask her would it be possible that she might have them. At least once a month there was some young fellow at my door, twisting his hat and asking if he might speak with me for a little.

After he'd sat down at my table and drunk a cup of coffee and stared out the window or up at the ceiling like he'd find the right words written there, and inquired about my health, and passed a few words about the crops and the weather, it would finally come out that he had heard that in some cases I had been willing to speak for a young man regarding certain matters, when a man could not rightly speak out himself.

With the ones I knew I would hem and haw a bit to tease them, ask if they could be a little clearer perhaps on just what they wanted me to speak of and to whom, if they'd prayed to the Lord for a sign, if they'd seen a doe with a fawn cross their path lately, if they'd thought about waking up for the rest of their days to the same face on the pillow beside them.

I would get some queer looks then from the ones that knew about Barbara's last years. She never was a woman to bite her lip and keep silent, and it was a rare person in three counties who hadn't heard her tales about me. Of course the young men were far too shy of an old preacher to bring out any of that to my face, so they'd just flush red and go even more tongue-tied then, and I would sometimes have a bit more fun trying to guess who it was they were after. Often it was known right around the whole countryside, from the eyes they'd made at meeting or in town or at the conference. But other times I at least would have heard nothing, and then I would throw out some likely names, just to let the poor boy squirm a little more, and how their faces would go hot and their feet shuffle about the chair feet then.

Finally, after I'd remarked about the strange heat for September and how a man could scarcely keep his house cool enough for guests these latter days, I would stop teasing and ask them straight out who they had in mind. It was harder than you'd think to get some of those young bucks to say a name, although thinking on it now I expect they might never have said that name to another person, or aloud at all, though no doubt they had whispered it often enough, lying in the loft of their father's house, listening to their brothers snore, and dreaming of someone softer to share their blankets with, someone less likely to elbow them in the ribs for taking too much room or rolling a leg over in the night. One or two I would even venture came to me with no special one in mind, just hungry to start out and hoping I would mention somebody who might have them. Not that the young folk didn't have plenty of chances to see each other, at church and in town and even in the girls' parlor on a Sunday evening, if they'd been friendly for a while. Still, many of them were hardly ready to talk of anything more serious than the weather and the prospects for cattle and the new gravel road just gone in past their place.

And so they would come to me. That might seem strange to you, after all that Barbara and I went through. And I told them myself that I was not the man to come to for advice about women, which did not always stop them from asking, or me from talking when it came to that. But most wanted not my advice but just my services as messenger, and so many times I'd gone by now that the Amish boys within twenty miles had all heard of me, and any man with daughters ripe to marry knew what my errand was when he saw me come up his lane. It was a wonderful thing besides to see the young girls blush and drop their eyes when they saw me come to the door, knowing what my business was but not which one I was come for. Ah, there have been a few sticky ones, a few who weren't quite so happy, but God did not promise us that all our lives would be easy.

So all that was fine, and I would not be proud but I would dare to say that others have done the Lord's work less well and less of it too. But in the home things were not so swell. As the years went by and our children moved onto their own places, Barbara found being left to fend for herself three miles from town less and less to her liking, even though the panthers and bear were all gone by then and only a few wolves left in the timber who would never bother anyone. Finally I came back from a trip to Bureau County to find her all agitated and puffy, as though she had been holding her breath for three days and was about to let it all whoosh out, no matter what. She told me that she had spoken to our son Valentine about staying with him for a time and meant to go there so long as I kept up with all my travels. She'd come back any time, she said, that I promised her to stay home three months running and stop putting everyone else's business before my own family's, but if not she was bound and determined to spend no more nights alone in a cold cabin with only a dog and two cats for company.

Well, I tried quoting Scripture about loving your neighbor, and mentioned Paul and his travels, and our Lord Jesus himself having nowhere to lay his head, and should we not be thankful for having more than Him. But she just sniffed and said that if your wife was not your neighbor she did not know who was and that Paul did not have a wife and corn rotting in the sacks because it had never gotten planted while I was off on a tramp to New Orleans where the people could hardly be called our neighbors at any rate.

You can see how it all went then. I did promise her, and in all good faith, that I would do better. Then I went out and planted corn until it was stone dark and the rows so crooked I ended up turning half of it up with the cultivator. But not more than a week later a letter came from north at Princeton, asking me to come and minister to them while their bishop was laid up with fever and a wound from being gored by an ox. There were young people to be baptized, others to be wed, sermons to give, and how could I not do the Lord's work? Barbara did not even try to stop me, that time, but when I came back she was gone, with all her things, leaving the house clean as always. She left a letter saying she had gone to Valentine's, but when I went to see her she would not be moved. Stiff as a rock she could be, that woman, though I've been told once or twice that I'm stubborn enough myself.

I went to see her nearly every second week after that, on the Sundays we did not have meeting, rising early to walk the twenty miles to Valentine's farm on the Delavan Prairie. And she would act glad enough to see me, and we would sit together on the porch with the grandchildren around us and drink some lemonade and talk with Valentine and his Elizabeth about the crops and the gossip. Sometimes she would let me stay the night, just for the company, and we would lay our old gray heads together on the pillows and talk half the night about how we had come to this. But in the morning I'd be needing to get back, and when I'd ask her if this time she wouldn't come with me she'd say, "Na, Peter, my home is where I know there will be a man in the house every night and every morning. Besides, Elizabeth needs my help with the little ones. You can surely tend to yourself by now." Then she would wish me Godspeed and say goodbye without a tear. I would watch her turn and go back in, bent just a little and slow on her feet now, and then I would set out on the trail for my home, where the fireplace would be cold and the mice nibbling in the flour again.

And who is to say that she was wrong, my Barbara. For when the Lord took her it was all of a sudden, and me off at Partridge Creek for a week of meetings, so that I got back on a Friday in the early fall, just before the corn harvest, to find that she'd been gone two days already and with the heat they were already thinking that unless I came that day they would have to put her in the ground without me. So pale and quiet she looked when I took my farewell, the fire that had burned so bright in her all passed and gone. If there is any justice in God's green world she is surely seated at the highest table in heaven right now, where she'll never again fix me a meal by lamplight while I sit at table to tell her of my travels, or take the boys out with her to husk the corn or lay up the hay because their fool of a father is off again on his idea of the Lord's work.

So, would I do it again? Travel the world from Alsace to Canada to Ohio to Illinois, with more side trips and expeditions along the way than I can remember myself? Na, I suppose if you wanted to put one kind of face on it you could just say I was never satisfied. At least for years wherever I was seemed not so sweet as the place just over the hill and around the bend. I know we're to be content with what we have, and trust me, I prayed to God to make me so, and I wasn't like some I know always wanting more land or a prettier horse or even women other than their wives; for all the troubles Barbara and I had I never touched another, though I cannot say my eyes have never strayed.

The wanderlust, yes, I had a case of that and sure enough. But I might have run off and become a pirate or a cowboy or a desperado, yes? All of my going this place and that was for the Lord and His people, and badly in need of my humble counsel and admonition some of them were too, and grateful always, almost at least, they were for my coming and unhappy to see me go, unless there are more and better dissemblers in this vale of tears than this poor sinner has ever been able to discern.

So I went along until here I am, bent but not broken, spending half my days abed in my son's house, too creaky and feeble to get to church, let alone walk to Hopedale to see my grandchildren. I still think that someday I will make one last trip to New Orleans or Kentucky, but the call has not come and I know now that it may not come again. So it seems that my travels are over and my people too seem mostly settled and busy putting in and taking off and building bigger barns. It is a wonder to see how the land has changed, with the new straight roads and the fences and the prairies almost gone now for corn and wheat and the towns grown up where I remember land so wild and rough you'd never think there was another Christian in a hundred miles.

And then maybe over a rise I would spy a curl of smoke, and head that way, and there would be a field of girdled trees all gray and trashy with the straggly corn below them, and a fence of split rails around the cabin and the garden with a bony cow grazing around it, and a woman churning butter in the yard and her baby squalling by her. And I'd go up and ask for a night in the barn and a meal if they could spare it, and she would rub her hair back from her forehead with a dirty sleeve and pick the baby up to soothe it and say she supposed they could find a little something.

If she and her man were sociable we would sit at table and exchange the news, and tell our stories, and I would tell what God had done for me. And they would look at me, all dust and tatters from the road, my shoes worn down to shreds and my sack with nothing but a Bible and a cup and a dollar in it. And then I'd laugh and say, well, na, he'll do as much for you. And they would laugh, and sometimes the little ones too. And before I would go off to the barn if there was one or the loft or the haystack I would ask if I could pray with them, and even the men who'd been pulling from the jug all night would not refuse me that.

I would thank the Lord for traveling mercies and for bringing me safe to the home of these generous folk who had shared so freely with me. I would ask that He might bring His peace and the comforts of His love to every city and town and lonely cabin in this wild and beautiful land, that the saving grace of our Lord Jesus Christ might come to every heart of every man and woman on this night, in the forests and in the prairies and on the rivers, from Waterloo to New Orleans.

A while back I heard a long-haired, obviously bright graduate student talk at a conference about the grid system and how it was imposed on the midwestern landscape. He pointed out, truly I think, that the Midwest was the first totally planned settlement of a territory in history: the land was divided not by river frontage, not into pieces clustered around villages, not by meets and bounds, but into the regular square-mile sections and six-by-six-mile townships that all of us in the flatter parts of the Midwest in the last century and a half grew up assuming was the normal and natural way that a countryside should be organized. That much is fact. This guy was also convinced that the circle is holy and the square profane, that the grid of township roads and forty- or eighty-acre fields was entirely a desecration of the virgin prairie, that the people who imposed it were grim mechanistic capitalists with no respect for the land or capacity for spiritual experience.

I found myself halfway agreeing with him. Yet I am sure, also, that the Strubhars and the Gundys and the Nafzigers were overjoyed to see the roads go in, straight and true and—more important—clear of the muck, so that they could get their produce to market and themselves to town without such a struggle. Eventually, as the temperance movement took hold, they were glad to be able to sell corn for a decent price rather than distill it into whiskey just because it was more portable. Old Peter would have dismissed as an impious and ignorant fool anyone who tried to tell him that only the circle was holy. His people built their churches on the square, and their houses, and their barns, and he would have argued that the temple in Jerusalem was built so, and the tabernacle also, and that what is in the heart and in a man's life is what truly matters, anyway, not squares and circles.

By my boyhood there were precious few corners of the prairie that weren't used for something. By the time I left for college the fields ran from ditch to ditch on most sections, often with only a marker post or two to separate one from the next. Nobody pastured out cattle or hogs any more, the fencerow had to be mowed and the fence maintained . . . and the neighbors were generally neighborly enough, unlike Robert Frost's, to get along well enough without good fences. There were fewer neighbors anyway, with the farms getting bigger, and many of the old houses were torn down, the trees around them cut and burned, the yards plowed up for corn and soybeans. A crib or barn might survive for a while, standing awkward and undefended on a tiny plot of grass. During the winter, if there hadn't been snow, the farms that had once been prairie wore an aspect of incredible dullness, all browns and blacks, tattered cornstalks and dry bean straw and open earth ready to be disked and harrowed smooth in spring for the next planting. Even the sparse trees around the farmsteads and the water towers and elevators of the towns, visible from miles away, seemed skeletal and lifeless. Only the cars on the roads, and the yardlights studding the horizon after dark, seemed alive. I was living in another state by then, but my friend drove a school bus back home, and when I said something to him about spring being welcome, he said that the only difference was that the grass in the ditches turned green.

Valentine Strubhar at about the time he took up the ministry (1893), with only a hint of his Holstein look.

Valentine and Katherine Strubhar in about 1940 on the steps of the Meadows Memorial Home.

Jacob and Magdalena Gundy's wedding photo (1869). Note her stylish buttons, collar, and earrings.

George and Clara Gundy's wedding photo (1904). They were married in her parents' farm home new Washington, Illinois. The planned group singing was canceled when a house guest fell ill; a group of young men who came the night of the wedding for the traditional charivari merely sang "God Be with You" and left. The newlyweds spent their honeymoon visiting relatives in and around Carlock and Danvers.

Top row (from left to right): Maude Gundy and Belle Gundy. Middle row: George Gundy with button, Will Basting, and August Mercer. Bottom row: Clara Strubhar and Rosa Kinsinger

George and Clara Gundy with sons Gerdon and Ralph (about 1913).

George and Clara's sign. The new wing of the Meadows Memorial Home was dedicated on June 15, 1952, as the "Rev. G. I. Gundy Memorial Addition."

George in his later years. In the background is the truck he used to haul grain to the home and children to Bible school.

Clara in her later years, shortly before or after George's death in 1951.

SIX

Successful Farming:
Jacob Gundy, 1893

Rounding the corner of the barn with the salt block I collided with George, running full tilt the other way. "Dad, Dad!" he yelled. "Ginger is having her foal!" He was off at a dead run. Now on a farm like ours there is always some animal giving birth; we used to joke that if we kept a farm yearbook, the new arrivals section would be as fat as the Sears catalog. Still, a new horse was not so common, and Ginger was not just a work horse but our best riding mare, and we'd paid extra to have her bred with the Ropps' good stallion. So I dropped the salt block where I stood and moved my old farmer's bones as fast as they would go across the barnyard fence and into the pasture. I didn't catch George—he had a good head start—but I didn't lose much ground to him either.

It must have been an easy birth, because when I got there the little one was already rising on its unsteady, lanky legs and shaking itself off, with Ginger nuzzling and licking at it—no, him, I saw, and a good-looking colt too, black against his mother's strong russet, hearty-looking even in his first few minutes on solid ground, with a deep chest and sound lines. George was touching and petting him already too, making Ginger a little nervous and himself a mess. "Dad," he said, "you promised I could have a horse of my own soon, didn't you? And look how beautiful he is! I'll bet he'll beat any horse in the county when he's grown! Dad?"

In raising children, I have found, there are times when you must stand firm and times when if you do you will just get trampled. Still it doesn't do to let them think you're too easy. "Well," I began, "we have a big tax bill coming due, and I had hoped to sell a fine young colt to pay it. Peter Schantz told me the other day that he is looking for a good riding horse for his boy . . ."

"Ah, Dad! Let those Schantzes find their own horses! I am fourteen almost, and a young man needs a horse of his own! You told me I could get one soon . . ."

"It will be a good year before you can even ride him," I said, knowing I was giving in already. "And there's lots of time involved with a colt. I would expect you to do all his care, feeding, water, and training too . . ."

Right then he would have agreed to serve as a galley slave until he was twenty-one as long as he could keep the horse. I didn't tell him that Lena and I had already agreed that the foal might as well be George's; it doesn't hurt a boy to think that his father can be generous once in a while, especially given how often we must tell him no. And George was a good boy, something of a teaser and not beyond slipping off to hunt crawdads in the creek on a sunny afternoon, but a hard worker mainly, gentle with the younger ones and respectful to his mother. And after all his brother John, just a little over two years older, had been saddling his own horse for a while already. Naturally every child that comes along wants to do what he sees the older ones doing, only sooner.

It was a warm day for March, and mother and child seemed to have come through with no problems, so we stayed there for a little while longer, cleaned up a bit, and then led Ginger back up to the barn so that we could keep an eye on her for a day or two. George was still bouncing like a hard rubber ball, more excited than I've ever seen him, trying out names: "King? Rex? Thunder? Lightning? Flier? Sport?" None of them seemed to fit, somehow.

"He's such a looker, maybe we should call him Pretty Boy," I said.

"Dad! Come on . . . he is beautiful, though, isn't he? Maybe I'll call him Beauty."

"Well, call him what you like. Run and tell Mother and then come right back out and meet me by the back shed. I want to get you and John started sowing wheat right after dinner."

He went off then, and I walked back to the shed to get out the little two-wheeled cart with its hopper and gears that would sow the wheat faster and more even than the best hand. It had been new two years ago, a couple of years after the neighbors started to brag about how fine they were; I've always tried to keep up, but some of this new stuff I have little use for. And this fine new machine broke twice the first year we used it—once just a cotter key, but the second time a main sprocket that we had to send clear to Peoria for, so that I just parked the thing in disgust and walked the field with a bag of seed as I'd always done. But last year it had worked without a hitch and we'd had the nicest stand of wheat I could remember. Now if only they'd invent a machine to cut thistles for us.

I uncovered it and started cleaning and greasing it up, and as I did my mind wandered back to when I was a boy like George, so eager to grow and start in at the things a man does. Somehow then what came into my head was the time I rode over to see old Peter Nafziger, the one they called the Apostle, when I had courted Lena for seven months and decided it was time to ask someone to speak to her for me, as we all did then.

Apostle Peter was Lena's grandfather in fact, though amongst all his nine children and their fifty-some children, from what I'd heard, he could barely keep their names all straight. Half of his life he had been gone on his travels, to hear some tell it, more interested in four or five lonely Amish way down in New Orleans than in getting his own crops into the field. But he was always willing when it came to speaking for a young man who was hoping for the hand of a girl. Some said he mainly liked the chance to sit next to a pretty young girl and make her blush by asking if some boy would have her, almost as much as he liked wandering on foot like some frontier trader, but I don't know about that. I knew he had preached clear back in the old country, and then in Canada, and in Ohio, and was still traveling and doing the Lord's work here, though not quite so regular as he had, being eighty years old and all. Still there were no flies on him, he was quick as a cat in his mind and always ready to set off down the road, or so my friends who'd made use of his services all said.

I knew enough myself about the troubles of keeping families straight, coming myself from such a jumbled-up mess. My father, John, married twice, and his second wife, Mary, my mother, had four Birckelbaw children from her first marriage and three with John. By the time I came along Father was in his middle fifties and Mother over forty, and my Gundy half brother and sisters were old enough to be my parents. We were living in Ohio then, on a farm in Butler County, and John and Barbara, my half brother and sister, were both married and living nearby. Ann, their full sister, had already died of a fever, and Joseph, their younger brother, had died years before, on the trek through the Black Swamp to Lauber's Hill, where they hoped to settle but only stayed a few months, just after coming over.

Barbara told that story once when her family was over for Sunday

dinner; Father never wanted to talk about those early days. In fact
he was not much of a man for any kind of talk, at least when I was
around. But then he was so much older than me and always busy
with a farm that seemed never quite to produce as well as the neighbors', though I never really understood some of the whispers and
nudges until much later.

Father never gave up hope of finding that perfect patch of ground,
that much is clear to me. He would have liked to be rich like the
Augspurgers and build a big stone house and own mills and distilleries and so much land that he couldn't keep track of it all. But for
some reason it was not to be, though he surely worked as hard as
any man. He was always arriving a little too late, when the best land
was gone and the rest priced too high to do more than make payments and get by. Oh, we ate well enough, and got by, and I dare
say it was better than Bavaria, where to hear Barbara and John talk
it was so crowded that a man did well to find twenty acres to call
his own. Mostly we counted our blessings and were thankful, even
if we needed a chart to keep all our relations straight, especially after Elizabeth and Mary Birckelbaw and my true sister Fanny all married brothers, the Reverend Michael Miller's sons, and Christian Birckelbaw married their sister.

Even with so many of us all jumbled together into one sort-of family we got along, mainly. There were tempers all around, though, and
when they got roused it was generally Father's children against Mother's and both against us younger ones—we thought of course that
we were the true family, younger or not. Then it would truly be fox
in the henhouse time, and more than once Phoebe and I just tried
to find a safe corner and keep our heads low till everybody cooled
off.

I was not yet four when we headed down the river on the way to
Iowa, too small to remember much more than the funny feeling I
got in my legs when I stepped on the boat and felt it wobbling under me, and eating something that one of my Birckelbaw sisters gave
me on a plate, some spicy barbecue that tasted good but was so hot
it made me cry. We must have made quite a group on the boat, our
family and John's; there were three children younger than I was. I
asked, "Where Barbie?" and Mother told me that she was staying
behind, and when I heard that I cried again. She was more like my
aunt than my sister, but my favorite just the same, always quick to
pick me up and hold me to her, as if I were some treasure that had
almost been lost. I would see her again, but not for almost ten years.

Mother would tell me during those Iowa years that Barbara had had her fill of moving, that she had said plenty of times that she hoped never to see unbroken land again, that civilized living suited her just fine. And surely Iowa was rough compared to Butler County; people were moving there in droves, because land was still cheap compared to Ohio and even Illinois, but for us that meant precious few improvements and starting all over to make a farm out of the bare land in what they were calling the Half-Breed tract, because there had been Indians settled there after the Black Hawk War of 1832. There were still some around, peaceful enough now, but mostly sad and worn-looking. Sometimes we'd see them pass by on the roads, and as it turned out the title to our land still belonged to them, somehow, and that was partly why we left. I never felt so good about what was happening to them. But I was just a boy and didn't know what I could do.

What I remember most of those years along Sugar Creek is that as soon as I was able I was put to work: there was always wood to be gathered and chopped and brought in, cows to be fetched home, calves to be watered, eggs to be gathered, the garden and the corn to be weeded, and a hundred other tasks that a boy of five or six or seven could do so that a grown-up's time could be spent at something else. Oh, I grumbled and complained plenty, and slipped off when I could to play in the woods or down at the creek with Fanny and my younger sister Phoebe, and then when I got older and Father thought he could spare us I got to walk the mile and a half to school, which was a whole other sort of labor in itself, one that I liked all right but never found right down my alley.

I remember years later when a skinny young student from the state university came around to talk to some of us farmers. He said that he was a student of rural lifestyles, or some such, and asked all sorts of questions about how we'd grown up, where we'd lived, what we'd done with our lives and such. He was from Philadelphia, as I recall, and seemed more or less awestruck by the work involved with getting a living on the farm. When I started listing off all the chores I remembered doing he wrote them down dutifully and kept telling me to go on, but I could see he had something else he really wanted to get at. Finally I ran out of chores and he asked me how I'd *felt* as a young boy about being worked so hard, whether it made me resent my parents or farm living. "Well," I said, "the good Lord knows they worked just as hard, or harder, to make a living for us. And they taught us that there was no point in complaining about what needed done, that it all went better if we'd just pitch in until it was over. And of course there were always Sundays to rest."

"But didn't you miss having toys, and time to play with them?"

"Oh, I suppose. But nobody else had such things either."

"And why did you decide to become a farmer yourself?"

I had to pause for a minute there. Had I ever thought about it really? What else could I have done? My half brother John had become a cooper and a preacher; I had a knack for working with my hands and had done some blacksmithing on the side. But I had farming in my blood, and started working out for a neighbor before I was out of my teens. I had rented my own place even before I went to see old Peter . . . "There's no better life," I found myself saying, surprising myself a little. "Springtime in the fields, with a soft wind and sunshine and the smell of new-broken earth, and the harness creaking and the horses plodding along before you . . . heading back to the barn at dusk, the sun going down all soft and golden, and looking back to see what you've worked that day, tired and hungry and sore but knowing that supper is on the stove and your chair by the fire is waiting . . . your good woman turning to greet you as you come in, and your children grabbing you by the waist, dirt and all. . ."

I could tell that my young scholar wasn't impressed by my list of simple pleasures, though to my face he was polite enough and thanked me as he shook my hand. It must have been a year later that a big envelope came in the mail with his report in it. Most of it was in words aimed at making a big impression rather than any sort of plain sense, along with some charts and tables, and I skipped over most of it pretty fast. But in the last part, which was labeled "Discussion," he went on for pages about farm folk who weren't smart enough to see how bad they had it, how hard their lives were, how abused they'd been as children by parents that forced them to labor like galley slaves, and how it took an "independent researcher" such as himself to "tease out the embitterment embedded in such cheerful platitudes."

I read the part about galley slaves and embitterment to Lena and the kids, and after we looked up platitudes in the dictionary we all had a good laugh, though one or two of the girls took it as a chance to say they *did* think that a new bonnet would make them feel less embittered. George said that if I was not such a cruel father I'd tell him to just take the next week off and sit by the creek sucking clover. "Yes," I said, "and I'll turn the horses out to pasture too, and give the cows away so we needn't milk them twice a day, and we'll all live on roots and wild berries, and pray for manna in the winter." For months after that, whenever somebody had an unpleasant job to do, or just wanted a little breather, they would say, "Pop, I'm filled up with embitterment over this."

I was still just a boy when Father died in Iowa—he just had an attack in the middle of milking one day, and the next he was gone. When he was decently in the ground, there was much talk around the supper table of what we should do. We had just found out that he did not have clear title to the farm, it being part of the Half-Breed Tract, though he had paid good money for it, all of which the agent had long since disappeared with, of course. So unless we wanted to go to court, which our people had never believed in, there was not much question of staying. Mary wanted to go back to Butler County, and Fanny and I, who were getting a taste for going west, thought Oregon sounded interesting. But it wasn't long until Mother got a letter from Barbara, who had moved to Illinois with her husband, Rudy Eyer, saying that she knew a farmer nearby who was looking for help and that we could stay with them until we found our own place.

This time I was old enough to remember the move. You learn who people are in such times, and I learned that my mother was a woman who could gather her things together and head off for a place she'd never seen before with less fuss and bother than some people devote to getting ready for church on an ordinary Sunday. We all helped, of course, but in no time she had the affairs settled, the stock sold off, and what we needed sorted out from what she thought we could spare. And I'll not forget rumbling across Illinois in two old wagons, with five of us children—Mary and Christian all grown, Fanny almost so, me eleven, and Phoebe seven—and Mother and everything we owned in the world jammed into them. From my perch in the back of the wagon I could see her in profile, a little hunched and almost round in her black cap and shawl, with her glasses propped firm and crooked on her nose, like a big, bespectacled crow. She used to thank the Lord twice a week, at least, for those glasses, and say that without them she'd never be able to tell her children apart.

This time it was John and his family who stayed behind; he had half a dozen children by then and had moved north to around Trenton, where he had a farm and clear title and had started preaching in the church there, so that was no surprise. It was not easy to leave them even so, but seeing Barbie again almost made up for it, even though she was busy with her own children and had little enough time for a half brother just growing up. And we found many others from the old days in Ohio had made the move to Illinois while we were off in Iowa. There were the Strubhars, John and Peter and Valentine, and the Michael Kinsingers, and Bishop Joseph Stuckey and his family, and Apostle Peter Nafziger and his big brood.

That brought me back to thinking about the day I went to see Apostle Peter. He teased around with me for a little, just for form's sake; he knew very well why I was there, since Lena and I had been sparking for the last six months and I had been over there to sit with her in the parlor almost every Sunday night for the last two. Still he wanted to know what might bring a strapping young fellow like myself to visit such an old pilgrim as himself, and then he went off asking questions about the crops and just what piece of ground I was farming and how my various relatives were getting along, just to keep me from getting to the subject. Not until the coffee was drunk and the apple cobbler eaten would he let me say why I'd come, and then he wanted to know whether I'd thought this through carefully, and prayed to God for His guidance and blessing, and thought about seeing the same face at the breakfast table every morning for the rest of my life . . . all of which was mostly to let him feel a little important, I knew, he who'd had as much trouble keeping peace with his own wife as any man around, with her always rolling her eyes as she explained where Peter was gone off to *this* time and the work he'd left undone at home. She had died a few years before, but had gone off to live with one of her boys before that, saying that she might as well live with a wild goose as with Peter, and the goose might spend more time at home.

Joseph did persuade Peter to speak to his granddaughter Lena, without undue difficulty so far as we know. And so Peter went off to the crowded house a few miles south of his own, where Michael Kinsinger lived with his wife and the nine of their eleven children not yet married. What happened then, just how he broached the delicate subject to Lena and her parents and how enthusiastic she was about the whole business, I will leave to your imaginings. The record is quite clear on the outcome, however; Jacob and his Lena were wed at her father's house in January 1869. She wore a stylish, dark dress with buttons and white trim at collar and waist, diamond earrings, and some sort of hoops or bustle; Jacob wore a suit with broad lapels, a vest, and a tie. Lena's family was Hessian Amish and long-accustomed to such worldly items, which also seem not to have troubled the Reverend Joseph Stuckey, who married even more couples than old Peter brought together. The newlyweds took up life together on Jacob's farm in Dry Grove Township nearby and began almost at once to be fruitful and multiply; their first child, Lina Emma, was born in December 1869, eleven months after the wedding, and four boys and six more girls followed. Except for Jessie, the youngest daughter, who died at sixteen of tuberculosis, all lived into adulthood and married.

Jacob and Lena eventually moved to another farm a few miles away, which they rented at first—but by 1895 Jacob Gundy's name is on 103.78 acres in Sections 28 and 29 of White Oak Township in the McLean County plat book. They lived on the edge of the little town of Oak Grove, which did quite well until 1886, when the railroad went around the town and through Carlock, a mile and a half away. The doctor and the stores eventually relocated there, and today there's only a grassy field and a marker on the spot, though the Gundy farmstead is still in use.

I did think it was a shame when the railroad went around Oak Grove. It was handy to have a store and the doctor so close, and the thought that our land might be worth breaking up into building lots and selling off some day had even passed through my mind. But that was not to be, although some of us went to meetings and tried to convince the railroad folks that we were the coming thing. There was money from back East involved in the whole business, though, more than we could hope to match. It was one of those fights that you tell yourself you learn something by losing, and that's about it. And of course the railroad was a great help with the marketing; it wasn't long until our corn and wheat went to Chicago in bulk, rather than to Peoria in sacks, and the price got better and the handling easier, too.

We had little enough time to think about such things anyhow, with the farming to do and other matters with the church and the like always popping up. Not long after we married, when Lina and Al were babies and Carrie on the way, the whole business between Father Stuckey and the Ropp brothers and Joseph Joder came to a head. Now perhaps it was Lena's influence rubbing off on me—she was Hessian and had worn buttons all her life, and even played the piano a little bit, without doing any damage to her immortal soul that I was ever able to observe. All the agonizing over clothes and jewelry and partings of the hair and such seemed a waste of breath to me, when there were good people all around wanting to do the Lord's will without fearing damnation or the wrath of some stiff old man with every move.

So we were all for Father Stuckey and his ways—after all, he married us, and never said a word about Lena's dress or her earrings, though I know some preachers who would have died on the cross before uniting any good Amishman with a woman so stylish. I was never quite so keen on Joseph Joder and his talk of universal salvation, though, and many of us at North Danvers felt the same. He was always going on about all his studies, and in the Greek this and in the Latin that, until those of us who spent our days plowing fields instead of books were half dizzy. I saw some of his poems in the *Pantagraph,* and he did have a knack for a line. The one about White Oak Grove almost made me cry, me having walked through those same trees many times, and never thought anyone would capture the beauty of the place in words. But even then he had to get into his complaining about the church and men making up hell to scare other men with and all of that. It's clear enough in the Bible, about the eternal punishment, and I can't see why with all his studying he could never see that.

All the church business was important, of course, but day to day it was farming that kept us out of trouble. It took years after we moved to Oak Grove before we were able to buy the farm, but by the time George was born it was a going concern. We grew corn, wheat, and oats, mostly, with twenty acres of pasture and four of hay, plots of sorghum and potatoes besides the kitchen garden, and were feeding a few cows to milk and to breed, two dozen pigs, and a hundred laying hens, besides six horses and two mules for field work. With the children so small—Lina Emma, the oldest, was just ten, and we had five younger—Lena's sister Phoebe stayed with us to help out, and then there was a young field hand who worked barely hard enough to pay for his keep. That made ten of us for meals, with the children bouncing around, crying and begging for this and that, and the women bustling around trying to satisfy and hush them. Many's the day I remember sitting amongst all that hubbub not knowing whether to laugh or to cry, to thank God for blessing us with so much liveliness or to ask Him that the next hour might be a little bit more calm than the last one. Not that I suppose he spends a lot of his time troubling himself over such petty requests.

It was a great day, at least I thought so, when we had saved some and borrowed the rest so that we could buy the house and buildings and a little over a hundred acres of the home place for our own. By then I'd been on the land for long enough that I felt nearly as married to it as I did to Lena, but it was not the same so long as I knew that the deed was in some other man's hand. It was a good farm, and in the wet years when the prices didn't fall too far Lena and I sometimes marveled that we had something left at the end of the year, even with eleven children and hired help to feed and clothe, besides ourselves. Of course there were also years when not a drop fell from June to August and the corn and the wheat shriveled and fired up in the fields and it was all we could do to keep the animals from sweating off all the weight they'd gained in the spring. But we have always gotten by, thus far, with the good Lord's help.

When George came out to the shed, he had cooled down a little, but was still full of talk about Beauty, how he planned to train and feed him and raise him up to win every race. By the time we had the seeder greased and wheeled out into the sunshine, Lena was ringing the dinner bell and we walked back to wash up at the pump by the back door.

Jacob was road commissioner for White Oak Township, served on the school board, and lived out his life without much external drama. When he died on a Saturday night in 1919, of "neuralgia of the heart," the paper described him as "a well known retired farmer at Carlock." Aside from the minimal machinery, the use of draft animals, and the absence of electricity, I suspect that by then his farm was much more similar to the one I grew up on in the 1950s than to the one John Strubhar and his family moved onto in 1838. By now another wave of change has passed; most farmers in the area farm much more land and, if they have any livestock at all, run a big, mechanized beef or pork operation.

I went to White Oak Township one summer, on a Sunday afternoon when the thermometer was crowding 100. I drove through the places my relatives traveled daily, wondering at how hilly and various the country around the Mackinaw seemed compared to the Gridley Prairie, thirty miles northeast, where I grew up. My childhood imprinting was of a relentless grid of roads and fields broken only by the trees around the farmsteads, and half or more of those abandoned, torn down, plowed under as the farms got bigger and bigger. It had been a long time since I had seen this river country, and now I tried to imagine my long-dead ancestors moving through it. I crossed Mills Creek just out of Eureka, with its gentle breaks on both sides, and the gravel on the shoulders was a brownish shade not at all like the limestone farther north. Heading on and rubbernecking I almost bit the guardrail just before I crossed the Mackinaw, where there were hills too steep to plow.

It had been another dry summer and the corn was spiked, firing at the roots, yet the land still felt verdant in its greens and soft tans, the long vistas that spread away from me in the sunlight of late afternoon. From inside the car, with the windows up and cool air blowing in my face, it seemed like a land of riches and deep dependability, a place where, as William Stafford said, "Wherever we looked the land would hold us up." Remembering my father's three bad years out of the last four, I knew he would appreciate the various senses of that sentence.

I turned north just out of Carlock (pop. 450, says the sign) almost at random, then slammed on my brakes to read the big white sign there on a little knoll: "Site of Oak Grove—Only Village of White Oak Township un-

til 1888." There was a healthy cornfield to the north, wheat to the south, and a beautiful vista with some trees and gently rolling land down toward the water tower and church spires of Carlock. No ruins, no reconstructions, not a single building, unless you count a shed set back fifty yards on the other side of the road.

There is a theory that because humans originated on the savannahs of Africa we still are instinctively drawn strongly to such mixed landscapes, with grass and trees, open spaces and shelter. Whatever the reason, I felt a rush of emotion as I stood there, on land that had quite probably been— for a tiny fragment of its long and speechless existence—a street where my great-great-grandparents had walked. Perhaps here had been a store where they had bought nails and sugar and pants, gone back now to some state not quite natural but nearly so. Somewhere within a half mile was the land they had farmed for the better part of a half century. For a moment the place seemed soft and inviting to me, ready to welcome one of its grand-children home, to provide me with a living that would have nothing to do with money.

Of course it was also hotter than the hubs of hell, and I didn't know exactly where Jacob's place had been. I was tempted to follow a lane that led back to the northwest, but instead I took some pictures, soaked up the atmosphere for a few minutes more, and got back into my air-conditioned car. A mile north was a fancy housing development, people who drive to Bloomington or Normal to work, and then a stand of big, deep old trees that seemed to belong in another state. It only struck me a year later this must be the remnant of the White Oak Grove that Joseph Joder wrote a poem about. In the small town of Hudson I passed a long row of mailbox-es lined up at the entrance to a cemetery, and my muddled ponderings on the symbolism of that image lasted most of the way back to my parents' house.

SEVEN

Signs and Wonders:
Valentine Strubhar, 1932

Valentine. What sort of name is that? Saint, third century A.D., Christian martyr of Rome, says the Webster's. I suppose that the first Valentine was martyred before the Emperor Constantine made Christianity into a department of military morale and therefore the name was acceptable to my ancestors, antiestablishment purists that they were. For me it calls up only cheap cards bought by the pack, signed one after another as fast as possible, stuck in the boxes that everyone in the class had dutifully decorated the day before.

Those families of what my kids call the olden days weren't committed to name originality, anyway; they tended to recycle names each generation. The Valentine Strubhar who is my great-great-grandfather had an Uncle Valentine; his brothers John and Joseph (who died young) had Uncles John and Joseph, and both their father and their grandfather were Peter. This meant fewer names to learn to spell, though it tends to raise the blood pressure of genealogists and family historians who are trying to keep all these dead guys straight in their minds.

But what is an exotic name like Valentine doing amongst the Johns and Josephs and Peters? That's the question. No, it's really not the question, it's just one of the pointless questions that you ask when you don't know what is really important. A Valentine by any other name would still have grown and lived and died, most likely, not too differently.

Valentine's father, Peter, came to the United States as a boy of ten; his wife, Barbara Sweitzer, was but a year old when her parents came in 1832 from the Lorraine province of France. Her father changed his name from Jean Suisse to John Sweitzer with the move; like the others in this story, German was his language anyway. Valentine was born in April 1859 in a log cabin

in the woods along Rock Creek; he died in 1941 in the Old People's Home
in Meadows, which was run by his daughter Clara and her husband, George
Gundy, a solid brick building with all the latest conveniences.

When I was a boy I never doubted that there were signs and portents, it is true. It seemed obvious as the nose on my brother Christian's face that the Spirit was present and moving in our countryside, the way the shadows of clouds move across the fields on a hot
summer day. I would be out hoeing corn or mending fence, swelter-
ing in the heat and humidity, praying for relief and ready almost to
sell my birthright for a breeze or a moment's shade. And then out of
nowhere a little wind would rise and the heat would ease and I'd look
up to see a great boat of a cloud covering over the sun, and round
about me I could see the edges of the shade it made traveling over
the corn and the pasture like the passage of a giant bird. And in the
sudden cool I would almost shiver sometimes as the sweat on me
dried, and I felt as if I had been shown again that His eye was on
me, that He saw my sweat and my labor and my every inmost feeling too.

Now understand me, if you will—I would not presume to say that
God sent a cloud just to cool me off or to give me a sign of His watch-
fulness. There were the days of course when no cloud came at all,
when I just sweltered so long as I could stand it or until Christian or
Peter working beside me said, Na, too hot it is to bake ourselves into
bricks, let's find a shady spot and some of Mother's lemonade. And I
would not put the Almighty God of the Universe at fault for not cooling my brow with a breeze. Still, such a boy as I was, and in such a
time, with the countryside and the church both changing almost too
fast to keep up with, I could hardly help but feel that I had been
born into great times, and even perhaps to do great things. And my
mother used to tell me of the great comet with three tails that had
been in the sky while she was carrying me yet inside her, one named
after an Italian named Donati, and how she would be coming in at
dusk from the fields or the chicken house and see it there before her.
She claimed that every time she stopped to look at it, with its three
curved arms no Christian could see and not think of the Trinity, I
would stir and move inside her, as though I could not bear the waiting, as though I were eager to come out and see this marvelous world
for myself.

All in all of course most of my days were just ordinary days. And
yet with the country so wild and unsettled, there in the timber along
Rock Creek, even ordinary meant something different. There were

deer in the woods and all sorts of smaller game, although we moved away before I was of an age to be trusted with a gun, and we boys had great times playing along the creek in the spring and the fall. But it was the winter nights in that cabin that I will always remember, huddling at the fire with my three big brothers for as long as Mother and Father would let us, then hurrying up the ladder to crowd together under our feather ticks in the loft. Our noses would be half frozen from the chill even after the blankets had warmed the rest of us, the snow sifting through the roof shakes, and the wolves howling out in the night like they knew just where we were and were only waiting for us to make a single mistake for them to be hungry and howling no more.

Well, we never made that mistake, if indeed the wolves had any interest in a meal as stubborn and stringy as we would have made. But if I so much as whimpered or mentioned them I would hear of it for days from my brother Christian. He was the bold and restless one in my family, always out front on everything. Years later in a magazine I saw a picture of a circus rider in a gaudy costume standing bareback on a horse, going around a ring, and thought of how Christian had learned to ride Old Sam around the barnyard, standing up on the back of that swaybacked, heavyfooted old draft horse, finally even getting the tired old beast to gallop while Chris whooped and hollered like a cowboy.

And then there was the day he begged Father to take him out with him to cut timber and then the rope broke as Father was guiding a log up onto the wagon and trapped him beneath. Only seven, still Christian managed to move the horses around, hitch them back up to the log, and pull it away before Father was crushed entirely. A hero he was for weeks, until the rest of us got plenty tired of his boasting about his great deed and using it as an excuse to avoid his chores. And then he got lost on the prairie coming home from town with a team and wagon and had half the township out searching for him, only to find him lying back in the wagon cool as the milkhouse, studying the stars and planning (he claimed) his route for the morning.

But with such things happening, who could doubt that God Himself was watching over us in those days? Surely it seemed some hand must be guiding all that was happening there on the prairie, with things changing so fast and everywhere progress of all sorts, people moving in and building houses and breaking the open wild prairies to the plow. Father would tell us that when he came to Illinois as a boy no one thought that the prairie land would ever be farmed, or be worth farming—why, anyone could see that the best land was along the creeks and rivers, where the big groves of trees were, not on those wide stretches of paltry grasses and wildflowers with roots so deep it took an axe to cut them.

That was why Father borrowed and bought land along the Rock Creek, with the big stand of walnut trees that everyone said he'd never pay off. He had it figured that the timber was going fast, scarce as it was in those parts, and good money was to be had both by timbering off his own land and by milling lumber for others. He was right, too. But he was also shrewd enough to realize not many years later that the future of farming lay out on the open prairies, where there were no stumps to contend with and the land lay smooth and flat for the plow. The grass once cut and the roots killed, he liked to say when he was an old man, that prairie soil will grow more corn than any dirt in the world.

So we moved from the hills and hollows to the big frame house on the prairie just east of Washington and the good farm Father had bought there with money from the sawmill. That was another great day. Springtime it was, a rainy spell, with the roads so bad it took four horses to pull each of the wagons the twenty miles through the mud to our new place. Father and Joseph, my oldest brother, had the wagons, with Christian driving the buggy with the old team and Mother, Peter, and myself. I remember huddling in that buggy, trying to keep myself dry and warm and accomplishing neither for what seemed like the whole week of Creation but was, I suppose, only a very long day.

When we reached the Mackinaw at Slabtown the old wooden bridge was creaking and rocking with the current, the water hauling at it like a living thing, so that Father got down and walked half across and looked for a long time before he came back and slapped the reins for the horses to take the first wagon across. Joseph's wagon was next, then the rest of us in the buggy, and we all held our breath and prayed every inch of the way, Mother calling out aloud to God to hold us up. We made it safe enough, praise the Lord, though even with the long spring daylight it was dark before we reached our new home. And the next day, there at our beautiful new house, we heard that two hours after we had crossed the whole bridge had torn loose and gone down the river.

Such a grand new place it was, there: not logs but real framed lumber with the clapboards painted white, seven good rooms and a real stairway up to the second floor, plaster on all the walls, and a fine tight shingle roof. No more snow on our blankets in the winter, and out of earshot of the wolves too. I remember, child that I was, saying to Father that we must be rich now. He muttered that I was not to be prideful and that we were far from rich, but I could see how happy he and Mother were too with the new farm.

So things were fine there on the prairie, with good rich soil to be planted and our cows and pigs doing well and myself just getting big enough to begin to help with the chores. Still, even young as I was I realized that we had moved a long ways from our old neighbors. On Sundays we did not often rise early enough to make the long drive in the wagon back to the Rock Creek Meeting. Father and some others had been brooding and talking too about the need for a church around Washington, where many more of our brothers and sisters had moved in lately around us. One week then in the spring of 1866 there was a great stir about the place, as Father and some of the neighbor men and boys left early for the timber and came back with a wagonload of saplings, three or four inches thick. Two days they spent putting boards across those saplings and making benches, which they set out all under the trees in our house yard.

And early on that Sunday the wagons started to come into the yard, dozens of them it seemed, and more people too on horseback and still more on foot. I was kept running to help with setting the horses out into the pasture and whatnot. But before long it seemed everyone was settled on the benches and the service began.

Being only seven myself I did not pay much attention through the singing and Scripture and opening prayers. But I could not help but perk up my ears when Brother Joseph Stuckey stood up on our little front porch to preach. A burly and a tall man he was, his beard great and full, his voice strong and deep so that it seemed the thunder was rolling out over all of us gathered there. I understood only a few of his words, but there was no mistaking the power of his spirit and of the God that he called us to serve. It seemed as if the very breeze stopped that we all might hear him well, that full rich voice rolling out over us gathered there under the shade trees on that beautiful spring day.

From my perch on the bench Father had made I looked out over the field that he and my brothers had plowed, the soil black and soft and ready for corn, and the pasture already green and shining with the early rains, and the timber with the new leaves shivering in the bright sun. And I felt myself caught up in something that I had no words for, and do not now, some tide or current or river that was carrying me on with all the others there about me, all of us together, bound for some place out beyond the horizon, some place in the sky. And Brother Stuckey's words were lifting us, and praising God, and asking us if we had love enough and strength enough to make known the word of the Lord in this new land and to give back to Him in praise some portion of all that had been given to us. And I felt then what has sustained me through my long life and all the trials and troubles to come, how great a joy and how rich a duty it is to sing the Lord's song in this strange and beautiful land.

Valentine Strubhar wrote a family history of his own, almost twenty-five typed pages worth, as well as a history of the Calvary Mennonite Church and innumerable sermons. I have used those documents more for what they tell about the events of his life and his own thinking than for his literary style, which is rather ponderous for my tastes. Even his good daughter Clara allowed that when it came to preaching "he was more slow than some but he knew the Bible and taught it." He preached for an hour to his family members on his last day on earth, eighty years old, quivering with conviction and age, in the living room of George and Clara's apartment in the Old People's Home.

Yet of course there was more to him than church. He was one of those who find themselves entangled in all sorts of little knots—intrigues, controversies, family tragedies. He made a good deal of money for a man of his time and station, enough that his semibiographer hints at some reservations about his willingness to deal close and sharp. He bought land in Missouri from J. C. Penney and then sold it back, so that he and his family got to know the great man and made money on the deal too.

If his public statements, most of them late in his life, seem a little elevated, it seems only fair to imagine him not as the dour and hoary eminence of the late photos, with his solid upright frame and fringe of white hair, but as a boy and a young man, serious in the old photos as they all are, but deeper than most in the eyes. One picture shows him at about fourteen, in a dark suit and striped bow tie, his hair sticking up awkwardly around his ears, looking resigned and patient as a good Holstein.

In his wedding photo the bow tie is white and his big, broad hands are spread, one on a leg, the other on the chair arm. His wife, Katherine Guth, stands behind him as was the fashion, one arm on his shoulder, demure and pretty in a dark dress with lots of buttons down the front and a big white shawl collar. He looks like an earnest farmer, as he was, but something in the line of his mouth makes him seem only two or three steps away from being an outlaw, a desperado, the kind of man who in other circumstances might drift away from home, work aimlessly at various menial jobs, end up on some dusty cattle ranch in Kansas, show up unannounced at a tavern some hot Saturday afternoon, blow three months' wages on poker and whiskey, get into a stupid fight over a bar girl, and be buried without a prayer or a name on his grave.

Could it have been? Well, it surely wasn't. If Valentine had any such desperate tendencies they remained well in check, subdued perhaps by the stoutness of his family and his loyalties to them. But such are the fabrications that too much coffee and silence and dwelling on old photos will lead a man to, on a Wednesday in late July in these last years of the twentieth century, with the Olympics on TV every night and me staying up too late to watch them, lounging in the new loveseat for which we paid more dollars than John Strubhar paid for his first eighty acres complete with small house and other improvements, trying in the midafternoon to penetrate the layers of time around these people whose lives persist and echo down through the spiraling years, and will continue to echo long after I am gone. Forgive my sarcasm and my vanity and my idle fantasies, Valentine. I believe. Oh help my unbelief.

It was only a few years later when the church members decided we had worshipped in houses and barns and groves for long enough. Now of course they did not ask me; being ten years old, I thought that meeting under the trees was just fine, with the ants and bees to watch about their work and the chance of slipping off to the edge of the crowd while the preachers were going on to listen to the older men and boys talk quietly about crops and politics. But that year was curious in all sorts of ways. It rained and rained in early summer, just after the corn was planted, so that what did not drown grew up choked in weeds that we could not get into the fields to plow, and that fall the four of us boys and the hired man husked a whole forty acres in one day and got only half a wagon of corn.

Before that, though, we started to read in the papers that a great eclipse was coming and the world might just end all at once, the darkness returning to reign again over the face of the deep. Well Father and Mother paid that no mind when it came to chores, of course. So on that hot July afternoon with no cloud in the sky Mother and Mrs. Malone, the Irish lady working for us, were in the garden picking beans and hoeing around the sweet corn.

I had been given my own row to pick, but had been watching a ladybug crawl over the leaves, so my bucket was not very full when I noticed the sky beginning to darken. I looked about and the strangest cast of light I ever hope to see was upon the buildings and the barnyard and the trees. The sun was still high in the sky, not like a normal dusk, and yet the light was failing fast, as though the sun were a great lamp and some huge hand was turning it down bit by bit. There was a stirring among the birds in the trees and the chickens scratching around the barnyard, and then I saw the cattle trudging up the lane from the pasture, thinking night had come.

I was staring about, fascinated, when Mrs. Malone began to shriek. "The trumpet is sounding! Save me, Jesus!" she screamed, and then went into one of the fits she was prone to, right there in the garden, with the whole world growing darker around us all every minute. Mother of course went to her, found the spoon from her apron pocket, and worked it between her teeth as we'd learned to do, and before it was all dark Mrs. Malone was well enough to be helped inside, though she crushed most of two rows of beans and did some damage to the carrots and cabbage. But while I went up on the porch, I stayed outside as long as I could, half frightened too, but not wanting to miss a thing such as this, which from reading the papers I knew might not happen again in my lifetime. And how can a ten-year-old boy, having heard the story a hundred times already, help but think of our Lord on the cross and the fearful darkness of that day, when the sun's light failed from the sixth to the ninth hour? I wondered if somewhere in the land a saint was dying at that very moment, in pain and torment perhaps almost the equal of our Christ's, and whether someday I would be called to die myself.

And so solemn and alone I felt there, with everything still and the birds all gone to roost and just the dim unearthly glow cast down from the rim of the sun that the moon had left uncovered, that I felt no destiny was too strange or unlikely for me, that I might found a church or die crossing a swollen river or be swept up into heaven with a great cloud of witnesses, all as God would decide. And I began to wonder if indeed this might be the time God had chosen to take all his children home. Just that week Father Stuckey had preached a long sermon on Revelation, and though much of it had gone right through my head without sticking as I thought at the time, I found myself staring up into the gloom, looking for great beasts with the heads of eagles and lions, or seals being broken, or stars falling into the fields around.

I saw nothing like that. Yet all at once the silence and darkness were too much for me, and I hurried inside. My brothers and parents were gathered at the table, a lamp burning bright upon it, drinking cold tea and talking, and Mrs. Malone there too with a cold cloth on her forehead, looking drained as always after one of her spells. When they saw me Christian laughed and said, "Na, Val, did you see one of your spirits out there?" But I just looked at him, then went around to Mother and grabbed her around the neck for a hug. She told Chris to hush and sat me down beside her and held me close, asking quietly how it was outside. I couldn't tell her how it had felt, but only sat there with her, close, until the darkness began to lift.

So it was that the eclipse passed over us, and the hand of darkness once more proved too weak to prevail against the light. I thought of that afternoon often in later years, when the way about me seemed black and grim and the path I must take all too narrow and rocky: that if my own strength was not enough there were others I could turn to for solace, and that if we stayed together and kept faith we could persevere until the light returned.

Ah, signs and wonders, signs and portents. There were giants in the earth in those days. The men worked dawn to dark in the fields, coming into the house only to eat enormous meals and go back out again; the women worked even harder in the house, slaving over enormous wooden stoves, washing vast heaps of laundry by hand, putting up acres of vegetables for the winter. The children labored beside their parents cheerfully and walked miles through the snow to school, with hot potatoes for handwarmers. Everybody who didn't die young became an earnest Christian and stout defender of the faith, made lots of money, moved to town, dandled umpteen grandchildren, and died peacefully in his/her seventy-ninth year.

So we'd wish it. And why not. Surely what the old sepia photos show is not too many removes from the truth, even if the people in them put on their camera faces just as we do, or tried. In those days of slow film and eight-second exposures a look of gravity and somber reserve prevailed, as the ingratiating smile does today. Still, I suspect that their camera faces were only one step removed from their real ones. If their children and their friends will not speak ill of them when they are gone, perhaps the reasons are sufficient.

Val Strubhar went forward to confess his sins and be saved in 1880, when he was twenty-one, at what has been recorded as the first revival meeting among the Illinois Amish. Preaching was by the ubiquitous Bishop Joseph Stuckey and his brother Peter Stuckey, minister of the East Washington congregation. Forty souls were saved, Valentine reported rather proudly years later, "which created quite a stir," though evidently no more detailed descriptions of the meeting have survived. Some were heard to mutter that such evangelizing was unduly individualistic and emotional, not fitting for the plain and humble followers of Jesus. On the other side, others were muttering that the church was spiritually dead, and without such conversion experiences it would remain so.

The rumblings over revival meetings were only part of the religious disputations that seem at this remove to fill the last half of the century. Among the Illinois Amish there were splits and schisms and rumors of schisms, partings of the way over partings of hair, new churches being formed to the left and to the right, some wanting more freedom and some more en-

*thusiasm. The Stuckey Amish had already split off from the more tradi-
tional Amish and were fast looking more and more like Americans, buying farm machinery and earrings and fancy dresses. At the same time, they
were learning from progressive American Christianity about temperance and
the End Times and evangelism; it's a big mistake to think they were be-
coming "liberal" in the modern sense.*

*Even the grip of German was slipping, the young people growing up with
the English in school and scarcely learning enough to read the Bible in
God's language. The year after he graduated from eighth grade at the Green
Ridge School, Valentine Strubhar started to teach a Sunday school class,
which became more or less a series of German lessons, some of the other
young people being already less than fluent in the mother tongue. The ex-
tent of his success is not recorded, but at best it was a delaying action.
His daughter Clara spoke German almost entirely until she started school
in about 1891; by the time I came along, sixty years later, my family spoke
no more German than we did Swahili.*

*There is no denying that those were heady times, though, for the Strub-
har family. New farms were bought, the sons settled on them, houses were
remodeled and improved—all the hours of sweat seemed to be paying off.
The family histories repeat it like a charm: Peter Strubhar left each of his
four sons 160 acres of the best farmland in the world. Giants in the earth.*

*And when Val Strubhar took a fancy to "one of the most charming young
sisters of our church" he did not go to an intermediary like the aging Peter
Nafziger, though Brother Peter still lived in what I suspect was cantanker-
ous retirement a dozen or so miles away. Instead Faulty, as his friends
called him, mustered up his courage on a beautiful Sunday night, took her
hands in his, and asked young Katherine Guth all by himself. In early 1883
they were wed and went for their honeymoon on a sled ride to Peoria. They
set up housekeeping in the old family home nearby, the one whose stair-
case and plastered walls had so impressed young Valentine, the home where
Joseph Stuckey had preached the first sermon to what became the East
Washington congregation.*

That first year of our marriage so many changes came along, we
could scarcely keep our breath among them—as if a spring wind had
come up and time was moving with it faster and faster, toward some
end we could not see. There was the farm work to do of course, and
plenty of that with our starting out on a new place. Then just in May,
with the corn almost planted, my brother Joseph's first son, Alvin,
was taken home, only a day after his second birthday. We had barely finished grieving for him, and Joseph not yet finished at all, when
in the heart of August his wife, Jacobina, was taken, leaving two girls

just five and six behind. And in November then it was Uncle John's turn, the first of our family to come over, the one who'd walked from Ohio to Rock Creek and back to find a place for us all to start out and then done two men's work to earn our passage. And how could this Illinois prairie be the same without him?

With so much dying around us, I was filled with joy and yet unsettled when my Katie said the next summer that she was with child. Could it be that children would be given to us, when so many had been taken? Was it right even to pray that we be spared the loss of them, to ask God for such favors when we knew that others had grieved so sore and weary and for no evil they could see they had done? We prayed long and often anyway, all that cold winter, that God's will be done but that His will might be to bless our house and those in it and to keep our children safe from all the perils that would come to them.

After Christmas we had snow and more snow, and then wind from the northwest such as I'd never felt. That was the fall that the old Apostle Peter Nafziger died, ninety-six when he passed on, and well I remember the stories he would tell of the cold in Ontario where he had lived, so cold as he told it that the breath would freeze to the muzzles of cattle and they had to be led into the cabins to face the fire and thaw out. Of course Brother Peter, though a godly man, loved a good story and was not always so particular about the gospel truth of it.

But this cold was deep and bitter enough for any man or beast. We kept the stock inside, with plenty of bedding, and only lost one sickly calf and a hen or two. But would you not know that it would be the coldest night of all, thirty-two below by the mercury thermometer outside the door, with two feet and more of snow on the ground and blustering about in great drifts everywhere, that our first child should choose to come into this world. With the weather so awful no help could come to us, and while I knew well how to birth a calf or a lamb, I had not had so much practice with babies. And the custom was not for the man to be there, or anywhere closer than downstairs with a pipe and a glass of whiskey if he used such things, when a child was born.

Still, with only the two of us there, what could I do? Katie had gathered the cloths and the scissors, and I held her hand as tight as I could when she screamed and cried and talked to her in the little spells in between, trying to act calmer than I felt myself, thinking over and over that something must be going wrong for it to take so long and that I had nowhere in this world that I could go for help.

If there's a record kept of prayers sent up in a single night in January, my mark must be on it, and near the top too.

But when it all was over our little girl was there, purple as a new plum until she too began to cry in the cold of the bedroom, for all that the fire was bright as I could make it. I soon had her cleaned as best I could, swaddled in the cloths and laid on my Katherine's breast. Then I lay down beside them, in the bed still damp with my dear Katie's labor, and we all three held each other, listening to the wind hurl itself across our house like it meant to pull us loose and send us back to Ohio or all the way to the big ocean. And we knew then that our foundation was strong, and would hold, and see us through.

I went the next morning on the sleigh to tell Father and Mother and have them pass the news along. They told me that my grandfather Sweitzer had passed from this world in the night, not far from the time when our little Clara was coming into it. An old man he was, and ready in his heart to go, and yet it seemed then to me that so many of the old men were passing from us before the rest of us were ready to go on without them. Grandfather with his white chin whiskers and his stout frame had come himself across the water as a young man and made a place for himself in the New World, a place that now would be empty unless we could somehow fill it up.

In 1892 Val Strubhar and some Stuckey Amish leaders started working with the Railroad Schoolhouse nearby, holding Sunday schools and revivals for a group of church members living southwest of Washington between Pekin and Tremont. In the same year Rev. David Augspurger of Valentine's East Washington church moved to Aurora, Nebraska. When the Reverend Jacob Unsicker of East Washington passed on in 1893, the sole remaining pastor, Michael Kinsinger, wanted help. He called for a vote to select another minister, with the understanding that unless two-thirds of the members cast ballots, no minister would be appointed. After the three weeks allowed, Reverend Kinsinger announced that the lot had fallen upon Valentine Strubhar.

Well I was not convinced that the church was ready for an assistant pastor in any case. And then Brother Kinsinger said from the preacher's stand that I should be the one, even though I had but sixteen or seventeen votes, only one more than Brother John Nafziger, and that from two hundred and twenty-five members, most of them not even bothering to vote. Well I was surprised first of all, and flattered some that a few people thought so much of me, but sixteen votes from the whole church seemed hardly enough to pick someone to clean the place, let alone to preach the sacred Word. So I said that surely this was no call I could accept, for what seemed to me good reasons and plenty.

Yet Brother Kinsinger would not let me go. That whole autumn long he brought up the case every Sunday, how greatly he hoped and prayed that Brother Strubhar would see his way free of all human pride and striving to take up the charge and serve God's people to the best of his ability, and all the rest. So persistent in his gruff way the old man was that I did not know what to think. I tried to talk with my brothers and my parents and others in the church, but it seemed they had all gotten together secretly and agreed to give me no help one way or the other. "I am no speaker," I told them, over and over, "and you who know me know that well enough. Others know the Bible better, others have lived better lives, anyone else would be more suited to visiting the sick and the old. And so much work I have to do, that I might return more to the Lord from the fruits he has blessed me with. Cannot a man love the Lord and yet leave some tasks to those whose gifts are greater?"

Even my dear Katie only nodded when I told her all my reasons. "Na, Faulty, I love you and will stand by you. Surely it is true that much has been given us to do and to have and to share. I would hate to see you gone so much on church business as a preacher must be, that is true. . . . And yet I remember our Lord saying that he must be about his Father's business. I suppose you must decide."

That Kate. She could sit for half an hour and listen, not speaking a word, and then say four sentences so mild and meek you would think butter would stay fresh in her mouth for a week, and when she was done I would be hanging my head like a dog that has stolen a chicken from the coop. So I asked her just how she thought all my work would get done if I took on the church work too, with only the girls to help out around the place and hired hands more expensive and more shiftless every year. And I asked her if she were ready to give up this fine house and move back into a log cabin in the timber, so that I could be about our Father's business. And being my Kate she did not argue or make plans or tell me just how it all could be done, but agreed and agreed that all these were problems until she had nearly agreed me to death.

I prayed long and hard that afternoon, asking for a sign, and along about dusk I walked alone through the fields and the timber as I had in my childhood, looking out for something in God's creation that would tell me what I should do. The trees were all bare, the downed leaves rustling as I stirred them with my boots, squirrels dashing around in the branches, and a great crow lifting from his branch with a squawk of complaint as I passed by. The creek was low and almost clear, the sticktights gone to seed everywhere, and a few tiny purple blossoms lingering in a low spot. In the low sun the earth seemed all made of gold, burnished like a lamp, glowing with the peace of fall and the harvest safely home. It seemed to be calling me to rest, and yet here was Brother Kinsinger calling me to give up the little rest I had.

I walked along until it was full dark and I knew Kate would be expecting me for supper, watching the first stars, hearing the late birds flutter in the thickets. And I called out to God for a sign, something bold and real that I could tell the others I had seen, something I could not mistake. But there was no great comet in the sky, no darkening of the sun in the broad afternoon. Only the dark coming on and a quarter moon rising above the shocks of corn and a rabbit scampering off to hide in the field.

Unable to come to any conclusion, Val Strubhar asked everyone in the congregation to come to the annual business meeting and to release him from his "perplexing position" in one way or the other. Here in his own words is his account of the crucial meeting:

On the tenth day of January 1893 a very cold day, a large congregation gathered in the church. Brother Peter Schantz was with us. Brother Kinsinger opened the meeting with a song and scripture reading and a prayer, in which he asked the Lord to help me to be willing to accept the call. After the preliminaries, Brother Kinsinger again arose and gave the object of the meeting urging me again to accept the call. He asked me if I had any thing to say, I should take the opportunity to do so, which I did. I told the congregation that under the present condition, with so little interest shown by the members of the church, I could not accept so sacred a call as the ministry.

There seemed to come a holy hush over the whole congregation, and for a few minutes there was a stillness that could almost be felt. No one uttered a word. Finally Brother Schantz got up and spoke a little while to the members, and then he turned to me and asked me this important question, "Brother Strubhar, if this congregation is unanimous in giving you the call, will you then be willing to accept it?" I replied, that if the congregation would give me their unanimous support, then with God's help and the aid of the Holy Spirit I would do the best that I knew, but if I found myself to be a failure in the ministry I would want the church to release me, and give the church a chance to call another man who would be capable. The church was willing to grant me that privilege.

And so Valentine Strubhar, thirty-four years old, never having "given a public talk except at Literary societies," came up to the pulpit. The congregation knelt in prayer, and the Reverends Kinsinger and Schantz laid their hands upon him and ordained him a minister of the Gospel, an office he was to pursue with diligence for more than forty years in the same congregation.

When it came time to preach—as it did the very next week, the Reverend Kinsinger being absent for the dedication of the new church building at North Danvers—Valentine was concerned that "preaching the Gospel was altogether different from debating a certain subject, where it was not so essential to proclaim the truth." But he started in, in the fashion of his people and his time, and seems to have done tolerably at it. He had a year or so of reasonably smooth sailing, except for a severe bout of inflammatory rheumatism that kept him in bed for seven weeks in the spring of 1893. He used the time to read the Bible, but quickly felt restless and finally went back to work behind the plow, even though for the first few days the hired man had to load him in a buggy for the trip to the field. After this he gave up active farm work, though he kept livestock and a huge garden.

The easy time at church ended in 1894, when the problem of languages reared up again. All the services and Sunday school classes had always been in German, but now a group of younger members asked the superintendent, one George C. Wagner, for permission to organize an English Bible class. Clara says that the English class was "for some of our English neighbors who began coming to our Sunday School." Again, evangelism and tradition were at loggerheads.

Brother Wagner was willing, but Valentine found that "this seemed to hurt the feelings of quite a number of the older brethren and sisters as well as our bishop." He found himself and the elder pastor, Michael Kinsinger, on opposite sides during the year of trouble that followed, "and the church became an unlovable place to go." Finally in June 1895, "without a prayer or the reading of God's word," "our bishop with a large number of the members seceded from the church." They formed the South Washington church, which remained active after Reverend Kinsinger died and continued on until 1937. "This was by far the saddest experience in all my ministerial work," Val wrote. "So many of the members quit going to any church, and would spend their time at home on the Lords day, so the following winter after I was through with my corn husking, I spent about two weeks visiting those members, and urging them not to stay at home on Sundays, but to go somewhere to church wherever they could feel most at home and which they were willing to do."

Yes, the break in the church was hard. I never was one of those who thought that God spoke only German and that English should be kept for trading and news of the world, but neither did I think that we were so many that we should be splitting ourselves over every little dispute. I kept thinking that we would find a way to convince the older members that a class in English would not condemn us all to perdition and that the ones who were so hot for change might be a little less forward and in a hurry to see things go their way so fast. But I was not able to make any peace among them, and to this day I wonder how I might have.

To see Brother Kinsinger leave the church and me behind, after he had all but lassoed and dragged me into the pulpit with a rope himself—what was a man to think? I was left then after only a year of preaching as the only minister, with the whole flock under my care, and many were the nights I wondered why this cup had been given to me. And in Katie's family some went with Brother Kinsinger and some stayed, so that for years we could not gather for Sunday dinner without an argument getting started over German and English and about what it meant to be faithful and to be the True Church. But such are the ways of the Lord, we must trust, though stony and painful they are for us to comprehend sometimes.

It was not only in the church that our faith was tested in those young years. We had the four girls, Clara, Ada, Barbara, and Lucy, all before Clara was six. But Ada was never so strong, and when she and Clara started school we asked the man teacher who rode his horse out from Washington to the school each day to carry her along the two miles when he could. Clara never understood why Ada would get a ride while she was left to walk, and what do you tell your child in such a case? That her sister will no doubt die soon and that to keep her alive, God willing, another year you would do anything in your power? Well nothing was in our power to do, horse rides or not, for in August of that year, 1892, she was taken from us by the meningitis, and may God rest her innocent young soul.

And even harder to bear was what happened with Lucy. One winter day Katie and I had gone to help her sister and brother-in-law Mary and George Rexroth butcher a couple of hogs. We left our Lucy, who was five, at her uncle Joseph's, and she was out playing in the orchard with her crippled cousin Chester, who was just a little older. They were jumping back and forth over the ashes from some trash Joseph had burned the day before, thinking the fire was all gone, but a spark was left somewhere and Lucy's flannel dress caught. She panicked and ran and the wind fanned the flames until her dress had burned almost to her waist. Joseph's wife, Phoebe, finally put out the flames, and the doctor came from town and did all there was to do in those days. But in the week she had left to live little Lucy had precious few moments of rest; her poor legs pained her so awfully, weeping and cracking as they did, that long before she left us we knew that she must go, and we prayed finally that she would suffer no more.

So with our trials and temptations we kept on as we could and praised God for the good things that he gave us, which were many of course. Another girl we had, Ruth, and then at last a son, Lyle Valentine Peter Strubhar, born in the first year of the new century. We were able to build a house on some acres in town, with a barn and chicken house along the tracks of the Santa Fe Railroad, and not long after Clara married her George and they moved onto the old farm. George even traded his fine horse Beauty, the fastest at the Rock Creek Fair two years running, for a pair of draft horses and a wagon.

Outside of Clara, there was nothing to make George's eyes flash like a fast horse; he pined after his Beauty all those first years of their marriage. But it was not long until George himself was visited by some of the ministers and asked if he would come and serve the church at Congerville.

He had no call, George said when he came to see me, especially not to Congerville, fourteen miles one way from the good farm where he hoped to live out his days. So I told him of my own time and how hard I had resisted, waiting for some miracle, some sign. I told him of that cold January in the church, when I had spoken to the congregation and said that without a clear sign I could not accept the call. "In the hush that fell when I had finished," I said, "it came to me, as clear as the light through the windows: God may speak through His great works and miracles, eclipses of the sun and comets in the sky. Yet surely he also speaks through His people, through their everyday doings, their words and their hands and their hearts. His signs and wonders were still everywhere, could I but read them, and I should not expect another three-tailed comet all to myself, but should see His will in His people around me. And if they called me to minister to them, I should answer that call."

George looked at me, a little darkly, from under those heavy brows. "I'll think of that," he grumbled, "when it's ten below on a Sunday in January and I'm up before dawn to hitch up the team and drive those fourteen miles to Congerville."

"And you'll have been up half the night, burning your good lamp oil to study the Scripture for the sermon you must preach," I said. "And you'll be called to visit the sick, and the widows, and everyone else who thinks they need the hand of the minister to hold them up. You'll see less of your children and your wife, and they will wonder why everyone else's business must come before your own and why the work in the fields now falls to them."

George looked out the window for a long moment, as though he could see all the way to Congerville, all that road rolling under his buggy wheels time and time again. "It might be," he said, "that if I'm to do this work so far from home and drive so many miles, then the Lord is telling me that I should find a Ford to take me back and forth." So I knew then that it was all right, and that he would go and do well, and the work would go on.

EIGHT ⁓

In Search of George and Clara

I stewed in my office, avoiding everybody, playing computer games guiltily for hours on end. How could I do this? I was stuck between filial piety, my stylishly nihilistic buddies, and my own inability to maintain seriousness for more than twenty minutes at a stretch, tops. I had just been reading about telling simple stories, what happens first, what happens next. It's the current literary fashion, strangely enough, here in the last years of the twentieth century. In the story by Grace Paley that I was reading, though, the narrator says she despises plot, always has: "Not for literary reasons, but because it takes all hope away. Everyone, real or invented, deserves the open destiny of life."

A simple story. The open destiny of life. However open George and Clara's destinies may have seemed to them—and I suspect that for years at a stretch they felt more like draft horses than wild mustangs—in earthly terms all their open prospects have closed down drastically, with their mortal coils now long adjusted to small apartments in the cold, cold ground. It's only here on the page that they are still free, or something like free, or at least I am free to twist and change and warp the words I write about them any way my whims lead.

Well, sort of. George and Clara may be safely dead, but the people who remember them are still plenty lively, enough of them anyway. Those people know me personally, and my parents too. They are interested in this project—they help me out, tell me anecdotes, give me leads about other people I should talk to. They have firm and clear ideas of who George and Clara were and how they should be remembered. How can I betray them? How can I not betray everybody? I have pictures, I have stories, I have responsibilities, but what I really want is for George and Clara to speak to me, clear and definite. I don't know how to get them to begin.

George Gundy, a Mennonite pastor in central Illinois for all his adult life, died in 1951 at the age of seventy-one. His wife, Clara Strubhar Gundy, lived to be ninety-four, passing on in 1979 at the Meadows Memorial Home.

Is that good enough? When I asked for money the first summer the grant readers told me that I had a big project ahead of me. I soon discovered that I could fool them. I could whip something out in two or three weeks, a whiz-bang, not so cynical, even touching job, if I didn't try to deal with all this boring actuality, all this "life." George and Clara were back there over the borderline where life becomes History, memorable, every salvaged scrap imbued with meaning and historical significance like bread soaked in wine, or grape juice. George was strong on temperance.

I was pretty sure that George didn't think about History much, because I myself was living a life and I certainly didn't think of mine that way. Most of the time I was just getting through, waiting for it to be time to finish the day's classes and lesson plans and paper grading and sessions with students and committee meetings, go home and muck around in the garden, get the kids in bed, sit for an hour, go to sleep. When I got right down to it, I spent more time worrying about the wins and losses of the various athletic teams I rooted for than about God or Truth or Literature or the state of my soul.

I understood, though, that I might be wrong about George. Certainly George knew things. George spoke strongly for temperance. George did not approve of women's underthings being hung outside, nor of anklets for girls in the first blush of youth. George had Views about Issues, some of which I suspected he picked up at Moody Bible Institute during the little postsecondary education he had, and most of those views were two hundred degrees or so from mine.

George did not shrink from his duties. George knew what the good shepherds know: where the people sit and who is missing and who was out too late. The high school boys are up in the balcony where he can keep an eye on them and where their noise doesn't distract the others too much. He knows the sleepers and the yawners and he understands. Even Clara nods sometimes, as you would too, up since five to get breakfast for the old folks, do chores, clean up, the usual Saturday routine just behind and the washing, ironing, and mangling to be done tomorrow. George knows there are souls in the pews more in need of the Word than Clara's.

When he points upward and speaks people listen. They don't obey always, but they listen. And he can live with that: he knows somehow when to push and when to back off, so that for all his tight and fundamental thinking everyone I can find wants merely to praise him, to say how kind and sure and gentle he was, how steady and how good.

I thought of myself as a writer and therefore condemned to consider everything interesting, including lots of stuff I knew George would have never looked at or touched except maybe to throw kerosene and a match on it. I had never been asked to preach except once on the Thursday before by the Methodists; I turned them down, pleading inadequate time to prepare. I was so broadminded I sometimes wondered if I had any borders at all. I was impatient and sarcastic and an intellectual snob, as at least two students reminded me on course evaluations every quarter, although at least two also always said I was boring.

*George would have known what to do with me, but George was gone. It was me in charge now. I was the one reading through the old sermon notes and the yellow pages of the **Christian Evangel**, listening to the scratchy interview tapes, staring at the green letters on the computer screen that were giving George back to the world, somehow, sort of, maybe.*

I typed stuff all day, caught up despite myself. All these glowing reports about George and Clara were so inspirational they were finally depressing. Didn't they ever just tell people to get lost, leave me alone, didn't they ever feel anger that wasn't holy? It made me feel like I should change my life, start being kinder to strangers, quit feeling superior and sarcastic all the time. Surely there must be more to it than that.

2. CLARA

What you need, my boy, is to settle down a little. What's all this fretting and straining going to get you? If there's a story to tell, it will get itself told, one way or another. All those years we lived together, worked and prayed together, we were too busy and caught up in the next day's needs to brood so much about what it all meant, how others might remember us, what sort of history we were a part of. I suppose George and the others talked about such things at the ministers' meetings, especially after those college boys like R. L. started coming in, but even they had more pressing business most of the time.

You have to remember that I was over fifty when I started writing in the diary Babs gave me for Christmas. By then we were well settled in our ways and even starting something like keeping a diary seemed a big change for me. It took me a while just to understand how it was laid out—for the first four months I almost filled the page each day, though I wondered why every page had five 19s on it. Finally I realized I was just supposed to write three or four lines and come back next year to fill in the year and write in the next spot down, so I'd have five years all spread out one below the other when I was done. Well, didn't I feel dumb and embarrassed at myself when I finally figured it out, but then I thought that no-body would see it but me anyway, and so I just wrote a little in here and there where there was room on those pages. And now here you are with them on a shelf in your office like they belong to you, right there between the poetry and the literary criticism, reading back and forth in all my thoughts and dealings without so much as a please or thank you. There's history for you. You live for a while and then you're helpless and people take your things and do what they will with them.

I never thought much about history, not the way you keep brooding over it certainly. But if you want to know, I think now that it's what is in the diary, the work we did and the people we knew, the illnesses and deaths and births. I never had room to write all that happened, or much at all of what I was thinking, and most nights I was too tired anyway to do more than keep track of the main things. We'd been in charge of the Old People's Home for ten years and more already then, living upstairs in a pretty nice apartment, but with the care and feeding of fifteen or twenty of those old folks always on us, day and night, though some of them helped a good deal and we got all sorts of help from the church people around, too. Still it meant getting up at five or six every morning to start cooking, and more washing and cleaning than three normal households. We had a big old mangler to press some of the laundry, and that went faster than hand ironing, but you wouldn't believe the mountains of wash there waiting on Monday morning. And then it was cooking and cleaning for everyone, too, and canning fruit and vegetables and beef so that we'd eat during the winter.

George was a miracle worker at getting help and goods; he hauled so much grain and fruit and coal in that old truck that he nearly broke the springs, sometimes from far away as Indiana and Nebraska. People didn't have much money, especially in the thirties, but after he'd spoken with them about their troubles and the bottom falling out of the markets and the kids all needing shoes he'd make a few remarks about the old folks, how the Good Book said not to cast them off in the days of their infirmity and how he wasn't feeling all that young himself these days and surely hoped there'd be someone to care for him when the time came. The way George talked, there wasn't a Christian in three states who could hear him and not start feeling his own age coming on, and not think that he'd just as well start storing up a good deed or two in his own account. It wasn't that George was pushy or bold or that he ever took more than someone could afford to give. He just had this way of making people see the good work that was being done and want to help.

So they'd manage to find some corn or oats or a few bales of hay that they could spare, and if there was a runt pig running around the barnyard George would want to know what the plans were for that pig, and before you know it the truck would be piled high and one of the boys or a friend from church would be perched on top with one hand on a rail and the other on the pig. And he'd drive those dusty gravel roads home, just a little too fast as he always did, and I'd hear him turn into the driveway, tooting his horn, and go out to the barn to see what he'd brought.

Sometimes I missed a week or more in the diary and had to go back and fill it all in at once, and a few times I got on the wrong page and had to paste in a little slip to get things right. But it's there, the life we lived, everything you need to know.

I know I should believe you, Clara. I can even see you, a little, from the way you write "same old Saturday routine" or "did the washing and the mangling" or "Grandma Vercler a little better" or "Don was home. Roland's came" or "canned 50 qts tomatoes 5 qts peaches." That first year, 1938, when you were writing more because you thought you had more room . . . why didn't you keep it up? Buy a new book every year if you had to? That first month, why it's almost enough.

Jan. 1 38: Another year gone with its sorrows joys blessings & burdens. Sat. morning and a beautiful cold day after days of mist & very little sunshine. Baked 7 pies 8 loaves bread, rolls & buns beside cleaning 4 chickens etc. etc. etc. Kistler was off the job. Papa & Mama both sick with grippe. Warren & Kenneth Tapke came with a suitcase to go to Bluffton.

Jan. 2: A beautiful sunshiny Lord's day with a large crowd at church. A New Year's sermon. Gerdon's were here, of course, Bobby too. Donna had such a nice time with her "bebe" till she fell & broke it. They stayed for band concert at the church. It was real good. Leni Minni Lyle and Dean Raber were at church. Papa & Mama somewhat better. Wrote to Ruth Yeck.

Jan. 3: Don left for Bluffton with June Baughman Emma Detweiler Virgil Morris. Don Roszhart & Bill Ramseyer as passengers beside the girls. Another nice day and for once we hung the wash out on the line. We did the mangling. Got a telegram telling of Walter Zelder's death. Geo worked at his books and his play

house. The man came to see about the wiring. Got out some reports in the evening.

Jan. 4: Got up at 5 and did the hard ironing before breakfast. Had
fried mush. Then we worked at the mending, fixed up a com-
forter, etc. Myrtle washed the sun parlor windows. I had snuf-
fles all day. Geo took paper off at the house. Put up the living
room curtains & took down Christmas decorations. Wrote to
Rosa.

Jan. 5: A very beautiful day. We baked 3 cakes and cleaned up the
house. Prayer meeting in the eve. Harry B. couldn't be here so
Geo led. I didn't go as I had sore throat. Had quite a crowd there.
Gene Ilene has measles, also Carolyn Schaer & numerous cases
out north.

Jan. 11: Tuesday. Had pancakes for breakfast—good ones too. We
did the mangling. Then sorted clothes and did the mending. Had
fresh beef liver for dinner and it was good too. Sam Schrocks
butchered and Geo helped. Cut out a dress for Mama, basted it
up while listening to a HealthMore agent demonstrate his machine—a fine one. Went to E.S. Augspurgers for a fine supper &
a nice visit.

Jan. 28: A beautiful day with a chilly south wind. A very happy 53rd
birthday. Schrocks, Mrs. Oyer, Aldine & Irma Jean, Mr & Mrs
Emanuel Zimmerman, Gerdons, Mrs Gittinger, Tillie & Marie,
Fern & Herbie, Celesta & Mrs Vercler were all here when we came
home at noon. They had a lovely dinner ready. 2 angel foods,
cookies, fruit, salads, b. beans, beef, ice cream, noodles, etc etc.
Got a box of candy, pr pillowcases, $7.00, card & letters, towel
& wash cloths.

Jan. 31: Jimmie and Roger were not feeling very well. Were beginning to break out. Did our ironing and mending. Got ready for
butchering.

Feb. 1: The folks wedding anniversary. Butchered five hogs. Had a
lot of good help. Jimmie & Roger have scarlet fever. I left all the
work here and went to stay with Pauline.

*I know who most of these people are. Gerdon and Pauline are your son
and his wife, my grandparents; Jimmie, Roger, and Donna are their children. Roger is also my father. Don, your other surviving son, was in school
at Bluffton College in Ohio, where I've worked for the last ten years. Papa
and Mama are your parents, living at the home. Virgil Morris ended up as
the elevator man in Chenoa, and I dated his daughter a few times in high
school. I could go on . . . the rest are other residents of the home, relatives,
church members, neighbors, on and on, such a great cloud of connections,
fellow travelers, souls kindred and otherwise.*

All that is impressive enough, but I can't shake my literary training. I want to ask about your feelings, about tone, about irony if there is any. What's with all those "goods" and "fines" that day in the middle of the month? Was it all really so fine or is that your code for a day when every-thing just went wrong, the pancakes were burned and the liver wasn't fresh? How did you manage this great whirl of work and visits and caretaking? Did it drive you crazy to leave home in the middle of hog butchering to go stay with Pauline and the boys with scarlet fever, or not? Am I wrong to read a certain gleefulness below "I left all the work here"? Was it just all right to leave the blood and the mess of butchering behind, let somebody else take care of that and all the other usual duties for once, go sleep in a quiet house with only two sick boys to worry over?

Stout as he was to look at, George was never such a healthy man. He suffered from colitis almost from the time we got married, all the time that we were on the farm at Washington, and I feared more than once that he would just up and die on me, leave me with the boys and the whole place to work by myself. And there were seasons when I did most of the outside work and the kitchen work to boot, when he was laid up with another of his attacks. This was in the teens and into the twenties, no tractor, just horses, but I did just about every-thing there was to do. I plowed and disked and harrowed, cultivated corn, drove four horses on the binder, cut corn, shocked oats, and husked corn. Even when he was too sick to work long stretches out-side, George somehow kept everything in running order, and if I had a problem with the binder he would come out in the car—looking like death warmed over, sometimes—and get it fixed up.

Most days I was happy to be out in the open air working, with the horses nickering and the harness creaking and the rich black dirt opening up for the seed. I've always loved the outside air and never been afraid of work, which Papa and Mama always told us was the secret to health and prosperity and staying out of trouble and just about everything else short of getting to heaven. I did have some trouble believing all of that at times when I was a girl, but by the time I was grown I was glad I'd learned the habit, for I certainly had all the work I needed cut out for me to do.

Not that George was a shirker. When he was feeling well enough he would be out in the fields all day for weeks on end, spring and fall especially, and before the boys got big enough to help much. Sometimes he'd take one of them out with him. When Don was full grown he would still talk about George taking him out to plow. George would carve a little set of farm buildings out of the clods and tell Don to imagine that other clods and cornstalks and such were horses and cows. He would get Don all set up, close enough to keep watch over him as George plowed, then when he got too far away he'd stop and set up something else—maybe have him imagine he was Uncle Peter Garber and ran a Ford garage right in the middle of town.

Of course we got so much help from the church at Congerville, all the time George was preaching there, when we were still on the home place. It was just a mile out of Washington and fourteen miles one way to the church at Congerville, a long drive in the best weather in a wagon. George was quick to reason out that if God was really calling him to preach there, He must want him to have a car to get back and forth, and it wasn't long until he found a secondhand Ford and learned how to drive it. He loved to drive, George did, and the faster the better; we had words more than once about how he might slow down a little. We had an accident coming back from Logansport with some of the grandkids once, and I tried to tell George that if he'd been going slower we might not have hit the other car. Quick as a flash he said, "If I'd have been going faster, I'd have been through the corner before the other car got there." I suppose everybody needs to be modern, one way or another.

But the Congerville folk would come up, as I said, to help us husk corn and bring plenty of good things to eat, besides feeding us nearly every Sunday after church, so that most weeks we would spend the afternoon visiting and just go to services in the evening without coming home. It saved driving, but of course then the chores were still to be done when we finally did get home, and often the cows and horses weren't too happy about being fed long after dark.

George did have his temper—he could be plenty snappy with a phrase when he was roused. For all that he loved horses, he'd not stand for any grief from them, and once when he was unloading corn and the horse balked, he got a stick and started in on the poor beast something awful. I happened to see him starting in from the kitchen window and watched for a while thinking he'd soon leave off. When he didn't I went out the door and called to him, "George, leave the poor beast alone!" He turned and looked at me, the second time I yelled, and said, "Wife, go back in the house and take care of things there, and I'll handle things out here!"

I hardly liked to take that for an answer, especially from my George who was normally so kind and mild with everyone. But I just gave him my best sorrowful look and turned slow as molasses and went back in, lingering in the doorway. By the time I got back to the window he was back at the horse, but it was plain that his heart wasn't in it any more, and in a minute he stopped. Of course by then the poor beast was in such pain and so confused that it wasn't worth a thing for getting the corn unloaded, but I just peeled my potatoes and watched George struggle and never said another word.

By the time he and the kids sat down to dinner I had remembered a story that Papa used to tell. I asked Gerdon, the oldest, if he'd every heard the one about the farmer who taught his mule to eat sawdust. "No!" he said. "Why yes," I said, "every day he'd mix a little more sawdust into the oats, and he went on that way for weeks, every day a little more sawdust and a little less oats, and the mule didn't seem to mind." I paused and waited. "So what happened, Mama?" he said, and I could see George watching me too. "Oh, it was working fine, except just when he had the mule good and trained it died on him," I said. Gerdon thought it was pretty funny, and Ralph wanted to have it explained to him, and Donnie, who was still in the high chair, started banging on his tray, all excited. While Gerdon was trying to explain it to Ralph I watched George from the corner of my eye, his face set, not saying a thing. I didn't say a thing either, just turned a little while later and asked how far he thought he'd get husking the south eighty before dark. "Oh, it depends on the horses," he said, not quite looking me in the eye. "I think I'm teaching them who's boss one minute, and then the next I think I don't know myself."

The Congerville church was the first Amish Mennonite church in Illinois to be located in town. It started as a Sunday school project of the Danvers church in 1891 and was organized as an independent church in 1896, largely due to the efforts of Clara's uncle, Rev. Peter Schantz. The first full-time pastor was Lee Lantz, George's old schoolteacher and a distant relative through the Birckelbaws, but in 1905 he got a call to a church in Nampa, Idaho, and so he and Frank Irons called on George. "Why do you call me there? Any place but there!" George responded, according to Irons's daughter. But George went to talk with Clara's father, Valentine, who was persuasive, and George began his duties as pastor there in 1906.

I've driven those fourteen miles from Washington to Congerville. The road runs south and east, leaving the open prairie for the rolling country along the Mackinaw and following the valley; for a few miles it's scenic and varied enough to deserve a yellow line on the map, although there isn't one. There are still remnants of the old groves near the river; I was within a few miles of the walnut grove that propelled Peter Strubhar to prosperity during the Civil War, and I crossed the Mackinaw where Slabtown on the north bank and Farnisville on the south used to stand, where Peter's family barely made it across the bridge during their move from the log cabin in the timber to the frame house on the prairie. The store with walls made of sawn log slabs is long gone from Slabtown now, of course, and the bridge is sturdy, generic American steel. The little hollow on the south side of the river used to be Farnisville, where Peter and Christian Farni, the first resident ministers of the Mackinaw Meeting, set up in business in the early years. They did well enough in a small way, but in 1856 got tangled up with two French speculators, Paul Carre and Charles Boutchamp, who bought the Farnis' store and claimed to have a large inheritance in France.

Being of German and Dutch origin, none of us have historically been inclined to put much confidence in Frenchmen, or anybody else outside of our own circles. Those circles being so small, on the other hand, we have often needed to rely on the trade, if not the kindness, of strangers. And these Frenchmen were apparently impressive fellows; the Farnis loaned them money to build a distillery on the strength of their supposed inheritance. But in the Panic of 1857 Carre and Boutchamp disappeared and the Farnis were left with debts far in excess of their assets. Christian consulted his friend Abraham Lincoln about the case, and the great man is reported to have asked, "Did they pull the wool over your eyes?" rhetorically I presume.

Christian and Peter were entangled in various lawsuits for years, and Christian was caught once running an underground distillery, trying to make his money back, and lost another thousand dollars clearing that case. Peter died in 1873, and in 1876, after a trip to Europe in search of Carre and Boutchamp proved fruitless, Christian and his wife moved to Kansas, presumably in disgust. Besides a few rundown houses, all that remains of Farnisville now is a white, plain Apostolic Christian church, its people distant cousins of the Amish and Mennonites.

3. George

I have a group picture of Clara with George, two of George's sisters, and three others. I don't know what the occasion was, but she is a very young woman, the background is formal, and they are all carefully dressed, the men in suits and ties, the young women in light-colored dresses with fancy collars. The three men are in the middle row, the women in pairs above and below them. Clara is closest to George, although it's impossible to tell if that means anything. They all have the unsmiling poses of the time.

On the back she wrote the names, and hers is "Clara Strubhar," so they were not married yet. She looks about sixteen, which would make George twenty-one. To my biased eye (and my wife agrees) they are easily the lookers of the group; George is almost movie-star handsome with his dark hair, dashing mustache, dark eyes, and heavy brows. Clara's hair is a lighter brown, tied up and back from her face with a black ribbon, and her white dress rises high up her throat, both covering her neck and lengthening it. Her eyes are also dark, deep-set, her nose long and straight, her lips poised as though she would like to smile but knows that she can't for the photograph. She seems both poised and innocent, tender and sensitive and capable, not a tease but too lively to resist the sorts of conversations that other people call flirting. She looks to be the kind of young woman that good men will court earnestly, doggedly, even desperately. George looks earnest himself, a little impatient, poised for motion, his stiff collar turned up and his tie exposed all the way around his neck. On his lapel is a button bearing the face of what seems to be an older woman, although it could be Clara; it's tilted at an angle, anyway, as if he'd been turning his lapel up to look at it.

The whole group of us had made a day trip to Peoria on the train, to see the sights and eat a meal out; the girls did some shopping and we boys mostly tagged along, trying to impress them with our cleverness and knowing all about the city. Now Belle and Maude were my sisters, and Rosa Kinsinger my first cousin, so you can guess which one of that group I was interested in. Clara was as pretty as any girl I knew, and even if she was only fifteen she was smart and lively and plenty grown-up too. With her folks living over near Washington and mine just north of Danvers it was a bit of a stretch to get to see her, but there were the church meetings and the Rock Creek Fair, and a husking bee or social now and then, and I managed well enough, not that her father wasn't a little suspicious about such an older man courting his first daughter, him being a preacher too and not the most liberal of men. I spent a long hour in Reverend Strubhar's parlor once, convincing him that my faith was sound and my intentions were honorable, or at least that I was frightened enough of him to keep my fleshly inclinations firmly in check.

For all our somber looks in the picture we were light-hearted that day, with the harvest in and Christmas coming up and our whole lives ahead of us looking as easy and pleasant as that photographer's background with its vines and bushes. We had clothes on our backs and money in our pockets. We were young and strong and loose in the big city, walking the streets in a big, noisy group, convinced we could save the world and keep a little of it for ourselves. Clara kept saying that this was the best day of our lives and that we had to have a picture made to remember it, and just to tease her I said that we'd best be sure the photographer had a sturdy camera so her big nose wouldn't crack it. She smacked me on the cheek at that, so that I had to grab her hand, naturally, and hold it for a minute while I looked in her eyes, both of us pretending to be angry but really so full of each other that, if not for the others looking on, we would have kissed right there in the street. As it was August Mercer made some smart remark about not handling the ladies as we would some calves, but I just ignored him.

So Clara pretended to sulk then, of course, and to ease her out of it I took the little picture of her I'd brought with me out of my pocket. I'd talked her sister out of it weeks ago and put it on a button, and now I pinned it on my jacket where a flower might go—a worldly thing for a couple of young Mennonites to do, no doubt, but we were feeling reckless. And when we lined up for the group picture she stood there just in front of me, so close I could not breathe without the clean, warm scent of her hair filling my head, and it was all I could do not to put my hand on her straight, slender waist, just where it swelled gently into her hips. As the man was talking to us she leaned back a little and murmured, "Keep your fingers crossed I don't break the camera," and smiled in that way she had and brushed her shoulder and her hair against me just a bit as though by accident, and maybe it was, but when the man said, "All right now, very still, look at me," I had to say a verse or two to myself to keep from leaning over right there on the risers and touching my lips to that soft curve just below her ear. When I saw myself in the picture, so tight-lipped and solemn looking, I had to think how strange it is what goes on inside our heads, that nobody knows except the good Lord, and how much forgiving there is for Him to do if everybody's head is anything like mine was in those days.

Clara was still too young to marry then, and I knew it, but she was so lively and open and liked by everyone who knew her that I was deathly afraid somebody else would win her over while she was just being friendly. Not that she was loose or anything like it, but there were plenty of young men I knew were thinking what a fine thing it would be to come home from the fields every night and find Clara there in the kitchen. And, as I said, I lived twenty miles away and could hardly watch her every move. All I could do was bide my time and see her when I could, at a husking bee or an oyster supper, once in a great while at a party where someone's parents were off on a trip and we'd have a fiddle and a banjo and a little dancing even. I was never quite easy with the dancing, but we were young and it was just someone's parlor with the rug rolled up, not one of those godless saloons with every kind of desperate character all thrown in together like a practice for the eternal fires.

One night we'd walked out to the kitchen for a drink of water and then onto the back porch for a little air. A windy summer night it was, with the sky trying to decide if it would gather up and storm to break the heat or just grumble and bluster and keep the good souls awake instead of letting them get their rest for church. We leaned against the porch rail and listened for a while.

"So much wind," Clara said, "it's as though it wants everything to be somewhere else. But the trees just keep saying no, no, we like it well enough where we are."

"I like it well enough here," I said. "But I'd like it better if we could go home together tonight and stay together and get up in the morning and drive to church together."

"It's not driving to church you're thinking about, George Gundy!" she said, pushing me away a little. "What you're thinking about mostly means babies and diapers, never sleeping a night through, work in the fields and the house and the garden that never ends. I've seen how tired Mama is, and I've handled babies already till I've had my fill of them. Don't you ever think there must be some other way to live?"

"You mean like rich folks, with servants and maids to do the work for you? You know I'd hire six women to do your bidding, Clara, if I had the means. But if you want a man like that, you'd better cast your net a little wider, because there aren't many among the Mennonites."

"Oh, I know. And it's not that I want money or even that I mind the work. It's just—I don't know. Papa always says that when he got the call he did his best to fight it, because he had so many irons in the fire and thought he'd never prosper once he started preaching. And look at him now, a man everyone knows and respects, not for his money but for his faith and his good works."

I didn't like the way this was heading. "Surely you're not saying that you want to marry a preacher? You think I should be a preacher? You know how I am, Clara—I'm as loyal to the church as anyone, but getting up to talk in front of people has never been my way. Taking care of horses, riding, fixing things up—those are what I'm good at. I'd sooner clean barns for a year than preach one Sunday."

Clara turned to look at me then, in the half moonlight. I could hear the music from the front room and then people laughing and clapping as the song ended. She was so beautiful and serious that if she'd asked me to climb up the side of the barn and fetch her a lightning rod I'd have thought I could do it.

"Papa never wanted to preach either. But he got the call and he answered it. You're not a showy talker, but you're like him, George, you have the knack for helping people see what needs done and how they might do it. You make people around you better, somehow. I don't know if the call will come to you, but don't think it's just fancy sentences that make a preacher. Just don't close yourself off from it, George, if it comes."

Suddenly what I needed to say next jumped right out at me, so big and frightening that my whole body felt like it had been flushed with hot water, then with cold. "I won't, Clara," I said, "if you won't close yourself off from standing up together with me someday and then riding home to be with me as long as we live."

She looked at me even longer then with those deep warm eyes, all grave and quiet, tugging at her lower lip just a little. Then she kissed me, very lightly but right on the lips. I started to pull her to me, but she slipped away and laughed and said, "Ah, George, I'm too young and we're both too serious. Let's go back inside. They'll be putting the fiddle away before long."

Too serious or not, George, you got Clara, she got a preacher for a husband, and you both got all the work you needed and more. Long after you were dead and gone, though, Clara remembered the dashing figure you cut at the Rock Creek Fair, how you and Beauty beat the man who'd won the horse race three years running and made all the Mennonites so proud, which was exactly the word she used, indicating I guess that the humility tradition was fading in central Illinois by this time, let alone the old Amish suspicion of such worldly activities as fairs and horse races.

One of the last of your old cohorts told me about driving with you once from the Carlock church to the cemetery nearby, and that on the way you said, "Harry, you see that tree there, alongside the road? One night I drove the horse off the road and under that tree, and I kissed my girlfriend!"

Was it Clara or some other girl you were driving about with, before or after? I was on that road, not two months ago, though I don't know if the tree is still there; the odds are against it, fifty years later, but who knows. I'd give a lot to know the whole story, but Harry didn't know any more, and the chances are very good that nobody else who's left does either. Can't you help me out? What do you think anyway, having your little remark plunked down in print here like a leaf fossilized in mud? That's not even to mention the conversations at the photographer's and the dance, which I've just flat made up. It hardly seems fair, I suppose, but then I never promised to be fair. It shouldn't be so easy to be remembered, anyway, should it? Even the Catholics think sainthood should be difficult. You've got so many people on your side, even now, that you need somebody like me to remind them you weren't Jesus himself reborn in the Illinois coun-

tryside. *I'm your flesh and blood, George, and I am on your side. Besides, I'm still here. You'll have to trust me, though I wouldn't claim to deserve it.*

4. GEORGE

Once George started in to preach, he put his best into it. He studied the few books he had front to back, read the *Christian Evangel* and the other church papers whenever he could, went to the meetings at Winona Lake in Indiana, even took a course at Moody Bible in Chicago. He would sit up late on Saturday nights at his rolltop desk, with his glasses on his nose and his shirtsleeves rolled, and after two or three hours I'd go to bed and hear him rustling around for a long time after that. Finally he'd have his notes written out, a page or two on those half sheets of paper that he used, and the next morning he'd speak from them for forty minutes, just as though he knew exactly what he was doing.

Of course the dancing stopped after he started preaching. The more he read, and especially after he went up to Moody's, the more he thought that he had to stand firm against some of those modern ways. He preached temperance often enough and the other sins got their time too. It wasn't just preaching, either; he decided that it wasn't fitting for me to hang my underthings outside for everyone to see, so I had to dry them on a line in the bathroom or down in the cellar.

By the time they moved to Meadows George had pretty much made up his mind about dancing, and a lot of other things, as these notes for a sermon he preached on August 16, 1925, suggest:

Dancing—does it say in the Bible that dancing is Sin?
It does not. But it doesn't say that it is a sin to burn your neighbor's building down—
Dancing is an expression of joy.
Miriam the prophetess and the women who were with her danced in their joy over their deliverance from the Egyptians Exodus 15–20.
David danced before the Ark—(A time to dance).
Dance if you can dance to the honor + glory of God.

But mixed dancing—dancing of men with women in the way in which it is carried on today—is wrong. And it is the cause of untold Sin + Misery and is forbidden in 2 Cor. 6–17 where we are told to touch not the unclean thing.

And the modern mixed dance is unclean. It is immodest, impure, unwholesome. If any lady should permit any gentleman except her husband, father, or brother to handle her anywhere else she would be regarded as immodest.

No Christian can dance without suffering loss of Spiritual power and bring reproach on the cause of Christ—

Dear Young, Keep your Selves unspoiled from the *World*.

Is there harm in a Christian playing cards?

Yes. If we are to enjoy the fullest blessing we should abstain *from all* evil.

Cards are the gambler's chief weapon. More persons become gamblers through card playing than any other way.

It is almost impossible to indulge in moderation. With almost everyone that plays cards, card playing becomes almost a Mania.

There are too many good wholesome games to be played to waste your time with a questionable thing.

Picture Shows—are a Menace to the Church and Country.

It could be used in the doing of much good. But if it is weighed in God's Balance it will be found wanting.

Where you see one good wholesome picture there will be ten of the other—Showing such scenes as are immoral. And they have the tendency of leading into Sin.

I have no more use for this trashy literature, Novels, than I do for the dance or cards or the show.

Rev. 22–15: "Outside are the dogs and sorcerers and fornicators and murderers and idolaters, and every one who loves and practices falsehood."

You might just as well go and see the thing acted on as to waste your time and weary your brain reading it.

What do you think about bobbed hair? It does not matter so much what I think.

There is no doubt in my mind that God is displeased . . .

Do you believe in Women holding offices? I do not.

Neither do I believe in giving boy scouts power to tell grown up men what to do.

Those of us with graduate degrees and liberal sentiments can of course hardly resist chortling—if not moaning—at this benightedness. George was no postmodernist born too soon; he had no time nor bent for the arcane philosophizing and toying with exotic ideas and "trashy literature" that earns paychecks for people like me. He was part of the last generation of amateur Mennonite preachers, which meant that he was untrained but not exactly ignorant nor entirely isolated. He had his time at Moody Bible, where he seems to have learned about some of Schofield's precise if quirky ideas about the End Times. Along with the traditional Mennonite pacifism and concern for church discipline, somewhere along the way he picked up what at the turn of the century were "progressive" Christian ideas: an interest in evangelism, in saving souls, in "temperance" meaning rigid abstinence. And of course he preached it all. Mostly, it should be said, he preached good Christian doctrine, for the salvation and encouragement of his flock. The dancing sermon is one of a few such in the box that still survive, among hundreds on less controversial subjects.

The people who remember him say he was a good preacher, down-to-earth and full of conviction; yet the stories they want to tell are not about his theology but about his style: sometimes thunderous, more often warm and humane. Everyone remembers the time when his son Don and another boy didn't come back into the sanctuary for the second half of the evening service. George was up preaching when the other boy's father got up to find his son, and without missing a beat he said, "Jake, bring mine in too!"

5. CLARA, 1963

So there I was, in the bedroom upstairs that was usually the girls', taking my hair down for the night in front of the high, dark wardrobe with all the little blouses and socks in it. And something told me I should turn around and I did, and there was Roger's oldest boy, just looking at me there with my hair down around my shoulders and my nightgown on. Of course I was decent, and he was only ten, and yet him looking at me so serious and close made me feel something I hadn't felt for years, as though I was a girl again at the fair or a camp meeting, looking out of the side of my face at some boy and then giggling from the other side to the girl sitting next to me.

All he said was Goodnight, Grandma, and I said goodnight, too, and then he went off down the hall to his room and I turned out the light and got into bed—the girls were sleeping in the spare room while I was there, so that I could have the better bed, though I told Arlene I could sleep anywhere and it was almost true, rare was the day when I wasn't so tired by the time I laid myself down that I even had time to notice whether what was under me was the softest goose down or the scratchiest cornhusks.

Still this evening I lay there on my back for a little while. I thought about those days so long ago, about George at the starting line on his fine black horse, not making airs the way some of the boys would have but mighty sure of himself and happy to be where he was all the same, so strong and fast as he slapped the reins and Beauty took off with him like a dark thunderbolt. George's hair and mustache, thick and full, were almost the same glossy black as the horse. And then when the horses and riders all came galloping back around with George in front and the girls all clapping and shouting, knowing they were acting a little too worldly for their mothers but yelling for George and the other boys anyway as they hunched and flapped their reins and shouted . . .

And afterwards when George had his prize of two dollars, good money in those days, he came right over to me and looked me in the face and asked if I would sit with him and eat an ice cream and celebrate his winning. I thought for a little that my knees would give out entirely. But then I knew they wouldn't, and I said, "Well, are you inviting your horse too, since he's the one did all the work?"

And now George had been gone ten years and more already, and his great-grandson peeking into my room to see an old lady with her hair down. A year or two more and he would be out looking for a girl of his own. How many times had I seen it, the looks going back and forth and then the hands and all the rest yearning for a touch, a whisper, anything. These days the young men and the girls both might be too free with each other for my old tastes, rubbing and kissing at every excuse, paying no attention to an old woman, thinking I could never have felt such things or had forgotten all about them long ago. But I remembered: every touch, every line of feeling, slipping through me like rain down a window or booming like thunder in the night.

And how many new ones had I seen, like the one downstairs in the cradle next to his mother, wrinkled and tiny and all bound up still in their tiny selves, but the flesh of my own flesh, born of that craving, that touch, that loving pain. Even now, with each one my heart would catch and almost stop, it would fill too full for its own good as I thought of my own children dead and living, my mother and father, my grandparents, and all the others before. They were shadows to me now, lengthening and deepening like shadows in the old farmyard on a slow summer evening when I'd slip out of bed for a last look, with the light still wandering around the barn and the chicken coop as though it was looking for one more treasure, as though it was no more willing than I to surrender, to let the day be over.

I was in graduate school when Clara died, and drove the four hours home on a Tuesday afternoon, just in time for the visitation. She had been fading for the last year. The last few times we had found her napping in her chair when we came and she seemed a little vague on who we were. Of course, she'd been an old woman for as long as I could remember. I found myself thinking that it was not so awful that she'd at last gone on, smiling as I greeted my aunt and uncle at the visitation, then thinking that it wasn't right to seem happy at such a time. I went on into the next room and looked at her body laid out in the coffin. A blank solemnity came upon me as it always does at such moments, face to face with the mystery. Mainly I remember her pale, lined face, her lips drawn closely together, her hair in its usual bun. Her stillness was unsurprising but profound, sad but not tragic, like the last chord of a long, complicated, just slightly redundant symphony.

I left straight from a seminar in reader-response criticism, taught by one of the current stars of my department, a man who'd written one of the few books on the subject. He was loud, smart, articulate, funny, arrogant, a New Yorker who lived up to all my country-boy stereotypes about New Yorkers. We read the usual things, Melville and Wordsworth and Dickinson, but then instead of talking about the stories and poems we wrote out our personal responses, made copies for everybody, and talked about those responses. They were supposed to be about the feelings and associations the readings brought up for us, describing them as completely and carefully as we could. The result was that by the middle of the term I knew more about the personal history, family, childhood traumas, and sexual adventures of the other six people in the class than I'd ever known about any group of strangers, not to mention most of my family members.

It was strange, not especially welcome knowledge, accompanied with all sorts of weird claims, pleas, and reservations. The professor told us, as if it were a fact of nature, that a man's attachment to his mother was by far the strongest possible human relationship. The divorced woman and the gay guy recounted their difficulties in intricate, embarrassing detail, as did the woman who didn't get along with her father.

Among all their tales of traumas and disasters I started to see myself in a new way, as someone whose life had been so normal and placid that the others could hardly believe it. The professor kept intimating that I must be repressing something; I couldn't work up any worthwhile hostility toward my parents, I didn't seem to feel any great dissatisfaction with my marriage or desire to commit adultery, in fact most of what I had to say about most of the people I knew was more grateful than resentful. I was still puzzling over it all, trying to decide if I really did have all sorts of buried traumas that I was just too blind to see, when I drove the four hours home.

At the funeral I looked around at my parents and siblings, the aunts and uncles and cousins and neighbors gathered there, solid farmers and teachers and nurses and small-town business people. I had thought of these people as both gossipy and reticent, snoopy and reluctant to talk about their feelings, parochial and unambitious, whiling away their lives between work, church, and high school athletic events. I had been assuming that my path was taking me steadily away from them and that I would be happier the farther that I got. But it struck me then that I was extremely lucky to belong among them, not only for the material security of my youth but also for the vision I had inherited from those years of how people might actually live together in something approaching harmony. I saw them as having somehow worked out a way of life that included both community and privacy.

It seemed to me then that the lives of loyalty, steadiness, and faith that I'd seen these people trying at least to live were a fortunate conjunction of centuries of religious experience with some weird, still emerging prairie aesthetics, born of the flatness and blandness of our native terrain and our century plus of modest prosperity upon it, something that only Easterners and city folks would dismiss as merely boring, although it is that too. I'd seen that it was possible to sit in a room with strangers as they talked earnestly and even with goodwill about their seamiest secrets and mine. But I was glad then to be back among people who, before they'd have done such a thing, would have stripped themselves naked and come to church painted blue of a Sunday morning.

The church was full for the funeral, though not so full as for George's; Clara had outlived many of those that might have come. There was a sermon, singing, a long drive from Meadows to Washington for the burial and then back for the meal afterwards. But the real service was something I'd never seen happen at a funeral before, near the end, when all sorts of people got up to say what they remembered her for. Mostly the stories were of gentleness, strength, work. What came back to me, for some reason, was a moment at my parents' house during what must have been one of Clara's last trips away from the home. We were sitting down around the kitchen table for supper, my brother Gregg and I both sporting our college beards, when Clara looked around at us, shook her head, and said ruefully, "My, you can't tell who the old men are here."

Her grandson Duane sang a song he'd written and played the guitar. We drove the thirty miles down Route 24 from Meadows to Washington and the thirty miles back in a chilly drizzle, we said our prayers and cried our tears, and yet the mood as it comes back to me now was warm and strangely easy, almost joyful. When we sat down to eat together there were many stories and more laughter than at any such time I can remember.

6. GEORGE, 1938

I tell you, it's strange when you realize that you're one of the old men, that the younger ones think of you as a stone in the road to whatever greater things they dream of, something to be gone around or rolled aside into the ditch or paved right over if it turns out you're too much in the way and too heavy and stubborn to root out. And no question there was some rooting out and rolling aside to be done among the ministers in our little Central Conference of Mennonites, especially in the twenties and after. That was when Clara and I had given up the farm at last, moved to Meadows to preach in the bigger church there and to run the Old People's Home, which was just getting started. We had fourteen old folks at the start, rooms on the second floor for us and the three boys, and a little dairy and a big garden, so it was more or less like being a farmer and a nursemaid and a businessman and a preacher all at once for me, and for Clara—well, she had nineteen people to keep clothed and fed and cleaned up after. You can figure what it was like for her.

That was mostly just work, though, not so much different from the kind we'd been doing all our lives. The coming of the likes of R. L. Hartzler and I. R. Detweiler and Harry Yoder was something else. It seemed like all of a sudden there they were, in the pulpits and at the meetings, filled up with their college learning and their seminary ideas, their Greek and Latin and more big words than you'd have heard from my pulpit in a lifetime, going on about eschatology and dispensationalism and all the rest. I'd picked up more of that lingo than the college boys sometimes gave me credit for, between my course at Moody's and the conferences and Winona Lake and all the rest. You can't preach every Sunday and sometimes twice during the week for forty years, all over three states, and not learn something along the way. But I never had the time nor much of the inclination for a whole lot of what they called higher education; there was always too much work to be done, and it always seemed to me that what the people mainly needed and wanted was to hear the Word of God as straight and simple as you could give it to them.

Not that I was always on the slow side of things. There were plenty of preachers with even less book learning than I had, most of them older than me. Clara's father, Valentine Strubhar, just to take one example close to home, could be as stiff-necked as any when the subject was one of the modern sins, the saloon or the dance or women on stage with painted faces. Still nobody could ever deny that he was a worthy old soul, stout and earnest as they come, and Clara loved him dearly, and so did I after a while, for all his pious ways.

And he gave up a good deal for his preaching; he was well on his way to being something of a land baron in those early days, from what I've heard, and every deal he touched seemed to blossom and bear like the ground cherries that covered our garden toward the end of every summer, no matter whether we encouraged them or not. Even later he bought some land from J. C. Penney out in Missouri, and we made some trips out there to see to it and got to know the great man himself—and a tight one he was, nearly had a conniption fit over a little length of fence wire that was laying around one time, told me to pick it up and store it properly just like I was his personal servant. But Valentine never did get rich, and by the end he would tell you that was all for the good. Some said there was just a hint of sour grapes in that, but I knew the old man well—and it wasn't more than a hint.

Yes, we had all kinds of contentions in those meetings, though as good Mennonites of course most of the time we agreed and praised each other to death on the surface. Even when we did get flat-out angry at the committee meetings, we generally papered it all over and tried to keep a brave face up for the people. I suppose that was part of Father Stuckey's legacy, that when you disagreed you still kept talking and tried to remember that the brother you were contending with was still a child of God—even though he might also be a pigheaded, ignorant, stiff-necked fool or an overeducated whippersnapper treading on the borders of heresy.

Father Stuckey had had his fill of contending, both with the conservatives—who wanted to keep to the old ways of dress and not use musical instruments or modern farm equipment—and with the ones like Joseph Joder, who was so far out on the liberal end that he claimed even the worst drunkards and murderers would be saved sooner or later, whether or not they repented of their sins. By the time Father Stuckey's contending with the bishops was more or less over and our church at Danvers and the others had decided to follow his lead, Schulmeister Joder was holed up in his study with his Greek and Hebrew, never to darken the door of a church again. And Father Stuckey mainly wanted to cease arguing about dress and machinery, but just preach the Gospel, praise the Lord, and build up the churches.

All of that he did pretty well, from what I hear and can judge, though I was just a young man when he was ending his ministry, right around the turn of the century. About that time the churches that had been growing up under his guidance finally got organized as a group. We called ourselves the Central Illinois Mennonite Conference at first, then just the Central Conference of Mennonites after the churches in Nebraska, Indiana, and Michigan joined. But if you want all that church history you can go read it in books.

What it meant for me was that the conference ministers started having meetings, and after I started preaching at Congerville in 1909 I found myself going to them three or four times a year. Mostly I enjoyed them well enough, especially in those early years, when we were all really just farmers who'd been called to preach one way or another and were trying to get on with it the best we could. Some of the churches were still calling men by lot then, but among us generally an older pastor would single out a young man in the congregation that he thought should take up the work and then stick to him like oatmeal dried in a bowl until the young man agreed. At least that's how Valentine got started, and me too.

And the meetings were almost like reunions in those times, since we were all related or had known each other since childhood, practically. Besides Valentine—they called him Faulty—my grandfather Mike Kinsinger was a preacher in the Hessian church south of Danvers and sometimes got mixed up with the other Michael Kinsinger who preached at Washington and drew Faulty into the ministry. And then my Aunt Anna married Rev. Peter Schantz, who was raised by the Christian Imhoffs, Clara's uncle and aunt, so he was almost related to me on both sides. Uncle Peter was a minister in the North Danvers church from as early as I can remember, along with Father Stuckey and Joash Stutzman, and he and Valentine married Clara and me. Then there was Lee Lantz, who was my schoolteacher before he started preaching at Congerville, and Emmanuel Troyer, who was ordained along with Lantz when I was nineteen, and Aaron Augspurger, who was Father Stuckey's grandson . . . oh, I could go on and on with these names, and I wasn't unusual. None of us could go to a church meeting in those days without every third person being some sort of relation or a friend from as far back as you could remember.

Things changed, though, as they will. People started to feel that preachers might well get some more training, and that was all well and good—the Lord knows how often I myself wished not to be so ignorant, as I sat there burning my good lamp oil after midnight on Saturday, thumbing my Bible over and over, searching the few books I had, and begging the Lord to give me some words to say the next morning. Then in the twenties the big Goshen College flap got started, when the Old Mennonite fundamentalists out East got so full of themselves that they closed the college right down for a year to clean all the liberals out of it.

Somehow out in Illinois we'd come to be seen as more liberal, especially us Stuckey Amish, and so we started to get some preachers who were looking to get away from the fundamentalists. William Weaver, who came to North Danvers in 1922, was one of that sort; he had been an Old Mennonite and preached at the Prairie Street church in Goshen and seemed glad enough to get out to Illinois where, he said, he didn't have to worry about whether his wife was wearing the proper bonnet. R. L. Hartzler came to Carlock from Goshen a little later, and I. R. Detweiler to Normal a little later yet, and then Harry Yoder—all of them good men, but they'd spent their lives, or at least the last years, mostly sitting in classrooms and talking and reading books, not milking cows and plowing corn. For us older ones it began to look like the seminary crowd was just about to take things over.

The worst time for me was toward the end of the thirties. We had weathered the depression pretty well at the Old People's Home, what with the farm and the dairy. We had never depended much on cash money anyway, and as long as I could get the old truck to run and make my trips out to pick up grain and hay and the occasional lame pig, we were all right. Still it weighed on you a little, an operation like that with twenty-some old folks all needing to be fed and taken care of every day, including the two smokers we'd fixed up the cobhouse for, and often as not a balance on the books of four dollars and some odd cents.

Faulty Strubhar and his wife, Katie, were long retired and living with us at the home by then. So the old guard among the preachers was men like Manny Troyer and Aaron Augspurger, both near seventy themselves if not past it, not that it slowed them down much. Then there were the college boys that I just mentioned, especially Hartzler and Detweiler when it came to pushing new things, and in between them some others like Earl Salzman and Ben Esch from Washington, who took over from Faulty there, and myself, who were not ready to go chasing off after every wild new idea but not beyond some listening either.

The meeting I remember the most was in May of '38. It was an awful time in the world anyway, with the depression just dragging on and on and the Communists saying that democracy was about to die out. All of Europe was in an uproar over Hitler charging this way and that, and some of our own people were even saying that at least he'd put people to work and was not a godless Communist.

Then, too, there were some who remembered the Great War and all the grief they had taken just for speaking German, let alone refusing to join the army, and the church at Flanagan had "Cowards" painted on it in yellow, and some of our boys were thrown into the federal jails and even died there just for obeying God's word that says "Thou shalt not kill." With all the different feelings and thoughts stirring, and the newspapers and magazines trying their best to get the war fever going all over, it was a hard time to preach the gospel of peace, no matter where you stood.

It seemed sometimes that if God had any sense he'd just wipe us all out and start over. And us Mennonites, when we weren't wishing in our darkest heart of hearts that He'd just wipe out the worldly ones and leave us alone, were in a quandary there seemed no escape from. Our people had wandered all over the green earth in search of nothing more than good land and a place to worship God without the government forcing our boys to go kill for them. Every place we had found, sooner or later, we'd been told that we must fight or go to jail or to the stake. We did not know what would happen if, or when, the government needed men for the next war, as it seemed it would soon. There had been some signs that there might be a program for our boys to do alternative service, but nothing was in writing. Where could we go next? There were not many places left.

So then when we get together, what do we talk about? Well, the Peoria Home Mission had worked up a little play of some sort that they planned to give wherever they could, to spread the Gospel they said. R. L. was all behind it and started in with his usual string of high-flown phrases and explanations so complicated that they didn't explain anything, wanting us as a ministerial association to support them in their earnest efforts to bring the Word to those still lingering in darkness, to find new means of reaching the unchurched and the lost, etc.

Now of course we had never had dramas in the churches, nor would any member in good standing have played a part in one. We thought even less of them than of drinking and smoking, which of course some of the brethren have always had a weakness for. In the old days when the roads were so bad that corn in the field or the crib was worth almost nothing, a good number of our people found that distilling it into whiskey was the only way to get ahead. Even Clara's great-uncle John worked in the Augspurger distillery in Butler County, Ohio, to raise the money to bring the rest of the family over.

But that was long ago, and in this civilized country I could see no use for whiskey except to ruin the lives of men and women and waste good grain that could go to feeding the world. As ministers we were mostly agreed on that and preached on it often and strong enough that the people in the churches pretty much came around to it too, although there was one stubborn old man in my church who would stand right up after I'd preached for an hour on temperance and declare that a little wine never hurt anybody.

It was dramatic pictures we were worrying that day, though, and not booze. With the war and all, my first thought when the subject came up was that such things seemed not to matter so much as they once had. Surely we had all changed and were not sweating over parts in the hair or buttons on clothes, and every one of us was driving a car by then. I might have said something and might not, this time. But Manny Troyer got up on his high horse right away about the evils of dramatic pictures and the sins of the flesh and the terrors of Hollywood and all the rest.

Before we knew it he'd made a motion, and Augspurger had seconded it, that we should have nothing to do with dramatic pictures. And didn't it get hot and heavy then. Detweiler, who loved nothing better than a good argument, started quoting Scripture in that way of his, twisting and turning everything, jumping from book to book and thought to conclusion until I at least had no idea what path he'd taken, though where he'd arrived was clear enough. It was, not to put too fine a point on it, that we old men ought to just creep off into some quiet corner and live out our hoary years in silence, if we couldn't wake up and notice that this was the twentieth century, and that the Gospel was eternal but in every age there must be new wineskins to convey it in.

That got my dander up, no matter what the issue, and I tried to explain to him and R. L. that some of us had experience that went back long before they'd been filling their diapers. If we had questions about starting some new program involving stages and speeches and the like, well, perhaps we had good reason for such questions. Beyond that we all knew that wine was a mocker and perhaps I. R. had best be careful about which comparisons he chose. Then Augspurger mentioned that his own grandfather Joseph Stuckey had been famous in three states for his zeal at spreading the Word and his belief in tolerance and diversity in nonessentials, but that he'd never gotten up and recited a stage speech or put on a fancy costume either in all his many travels, and the church seemed to have done well enough without any of it too.

So it was round and round then for a long while, with motions and countermotions and verses from this side and arguments from that. Finally Ben Esch, tired of the wrangling, made another motion, trying for the middle ground: "That we as the Ministerial Association encourage church groups with Reverend Hartzler who feel as for the interest and benefit of their own groups invite the group from the Mission field to encourage and stimulate Mission interest." Earl Salzman, who had been sitting there for the last twenty minutes with his eyes drooping and his head in his hands, said right away, "I'll second that!" And maybe because none of us quite followed just what Ben was saying, but thought it meant those that wanted the group could have it while the rest needn't, and because we wanted to get home not too long past midnight, we all agreed.

So after all that it was a long drive home, though the speedometer kept creeping up past sixty and seventy on me and nobody with me this time. I tried the radio but could only get dance music and shut it off after a few minutes, with visions of half-dressed Mennonite girls in the clutches of greasy, grinning, big-city boys running through my head. What would become of us, I thought. Here we were, not so far away from the days when we were willing to go to the wall over buttons, and now we were wandering down the primrose path toward who knows what. What would be next? Moving pictures in the churches on Sunday nights? Dances in the basement? Sermons in saloons? Beer and wine at the Fourth of July party?

Clara was long asleep when I got home. I almost woke her up, just to have somebody to stew it over with me, but she looked so easy and peaceful there with her hands under her cheek that I didn't have the heart. And then next morning there was the milking and the chores and the funeral for old Grandma Vercler to be done, and somehow I never found the right time to bring it up, but it all just kept circling around my head like one of those little whirlwinds that chases itself over the fields in the summertime.

What kind of church did we have? What had gone on in the days since Father Stuckey and the rest like him, the old men who had now gone on, the ones who had worked and struggled all their lives to make a church and a whole group of churches where there had been nothing but land left empty when the Indians were pushed off it? What did those men have in common with the new ones coming along now, with their fancy degrees and long sentences, and what could a man like me do to keep that old, true way from being lost forever? I remembered Faulty Strubhar talking of the day Father Stuckey spoke at the old Strubhar place east of Washington, how hundreds of people came when the word went out that they might start a church there on the open prairie. Faulty was but six or seven when it happened, but even as an old man he got all still and straight as he tried to describe how it was that day, as Father Stuckey's words went out from the front porch to the people gathered on the benches the Strubhars and their neighbors had cut and pieced together themselves. I knew as I listened that he could still feel the power of the Spirit as it had moved across them all, telling them that yes, it was time to make a new church and that yes, God would be with them.

Ah, but those days were gone, I thought, and those men too, or going. Myself I knew I never had such a gift for speaking, only what comes from being willing to tell the plain truth to those that will hear. The more I brooded the worse I felt about it all, the more tired I was of all the work and so little to show for it. Even right there in Meadows, I had just found out, the Sunday school teachers had organized some kind of "pageant" for children's day, of course without letting me get wind of it until they'd been practicing for weeks. When I did hear about it I gathered the teachers together after church the next Sunday and told them, as if they didn't know already, that I hardly saw the place of drama in the church, much less on Sunday morning.

"Oh, but Reverend Gundy," they said, so sweet I knew they'd planned it all out, just how to handle me, "the children have been working so hard, learning their parts, and it *is* all sound and Biblical, you can read it yourself, here's the script. Surely you wouldn't disappoint them so much after all they've done?"

They may have been talking to Clara. She had that way, when there was something she really wanted that she knew I'd not like one bit, of getting me into a spot where I'd be just a black-hearted monster if I kept her from having her way. Mercifully she didn't use it often, and neither did these teachers, but when they hit me with it this way, what could I do? I scowled and grumbled for a little about how it would never have happened in the old days, just for form's sake. All that did, though, was give the women their chance to start in to smiling and agreeing that yes, things certainly were changing, but wait until I saw how excited the boys and girls were about dressing up and putting it all on, and what a good message there'd be.

When I got the program for the conference that year and saw my name next to the main sermon, it was the last straw. The way I was feeling, if I got up before all those people under the tent to deliver the Word, I would be just as likely to find myself telling them all to get out the cards right there and we'd just have us a good clean Christian poker game right between the Scripture and the hymn singing. Might as well bring in the whiskey and the beer, get everybody who was old enough to walk roaring drunk, then fold up the chairs and let the men grab up the high school girls and each other's wives and dance them off into the bushes. Why not go all the way, set up a projector and a screen and have a picture show? And then when the war started we'd be all ready to send our boys off to fight and kill and die, and then the ones who came back would be just like all our neighbors, ready to go out and get rich and put up their big houses with slate roofs and two stairways, deal sharp and shady with everyone, and then go sit in the pew on Sunday mornings and expect to be congratulated for being so wealthy and blessed.

I'd never felt so convinced that the Devil was afoot—and so powerless to do anything to even slow him down. So I wrote to R. L., not a pamphlet filled with two-dollar words and twelve paragraphs of explanation like he would have sent to me, but this:

Meadows, Ill.
June 1

Rev. Hartzler

> I received the report of the program for conference and I see I am supposed to preach the conference sermon. I do feel that I should refuse to take that place. I think it would be better to give that place to some one else who can see the brighter side of our conference. I am sorry but I have lost confidence. So it would be better for all, if I remain silent and the rest continue to speak.
>
> Geo.

With the letter written and off in the mail I breathed easier, like I'd done what I could, and now it was time to let somebody else take over. I even thought for a few days that I'd settled it and that he could find somebody else to do the sermon. I would go to the meetings for once and just sit and listen and talk with my old friends during the breaks about the crops and the weather and who'd gotten a new car and who needed one. I would leave all the wrangling over doctrine and plays and dramatic pictures and war and peace to the college boys, who didn't think they needed our help anyway.

The children's program went on just as the women had decided, and the younger ones did seem to enjoy it, though I caught a few puzzled looks from the older folks, who'd never seen such a thing in church before and surely wondered just how I'd come to allow it. So when the sermon time came that morning, I preached on the gospel of love and the need to love pure and earnest and true as our Jesus himself did and to devote all our thoughts to his love and his saving grace. And if some of the old folks thought I was saying that the teachers should not push too far, I suppose some of the teachers thought that Jesus' love was just what their play was all about, even if they did have children dressed up as sheep and soldiers and who knows what all.

The next day came a big storm, enough to scare us all down into the basement, and getting twenty-some frail old folks down there without a fall is no easy task, let me tell you, with three of them so confused they're sure it's the Second Coming. One old man thought he just had to go out on the porch to greet his Savior face to face. But we got them all downstairs at last and rode it out, and when it cleared we found that two of our best sweet cherry trees and one peach were all broken down, besides big limbs out of the maples and all sorts of smaller trash everywhere. The cherry trees nearly broke Clara's heart, she had nursed them along so careful, but fruit trees in these parts are always chancy, I've found, except for apples. You coddle them and spray them and guard them from the rabbits, and still you get a late freeze or a big wind and then you're left with nothing but firewood.

The next afternoon I was out cutting up the fallen stuff, which was mostly too small to be worth much, when I heard a horn honk. I turned and saw Ben Esch getting out of his car, so I put down the buck saw and went across the yard to shake his hand. Ben had grown up in Clara's church in Washington, gone to school a couple of years behind her, and I'd known him for most of the last forty years. He had been Faulty's assistant at the Calvary church in Washington for some time and taken over as the main minister when Faulty retired. Like me he had farmed and preached at the same time and it nearly wore us both out. Ben didn't have the fourteen miles to drive, but the Washington church was bigger, and as he said, six twelve-hour days behind a horse didn't leave a man much time to work up a sermon or visit the sick.

For all of that, Ben had built up a fine farm, and during the First World War, when the grain prices all went up, he made so much money at it that he started to feel guilty. So he sold it off to a neighbor and used the money to study at Moody Bible College in Chicago. A few years later he decided his sons ought to grow up on the farm so he bought it back, but he had to borrow to do it, and then when the depression hit he couldn't come close to making the payments. After a while he finagled a job in town, managing the elevator, and they paid him $85 a month as long as his wife did the books too. That was

no less work and more aggravation than farming, and after Faulty retired Ben was expected to preach every Sunday plus take care of weddings and funerals and visiting the sick, and the church would take
up a love offering for him once in a while if they remembered.

So Ben knew just as well as I did what it meant to work yourself
harder than you would a horse that you felt the least bit of respect
for and get not much from it but the satisfaction of doing the Lord's
work. That's the way it was for us in those times, though, and we
didn't have the leisure to complain about it much.

It was odd, then, that he'd driven clear over to see me on a Tuesday afternoon, when he must have had work to do. I didn't ask him
about it right away, though. We shook hands and went in to get a
glass of lemonade and for Ben to say hello to Clara, who had been
out in the garden most of the morning but was in the kitchen now,
baking cookies and a cake along with starting supper for us and the
old folks. She promised us some cookies in a few minutes, and we
went back out to the porch to sip our lemonade and wait for them.

"So I hear you had quite a pageant last Sunday," Ben said, with a
little tilt of the head. "Your idea?" I looked at him hard, wondering
whether to get mad, but I'd known him too long to take his teasing
to heart.

"Oh, yes," I said, "and next week we're having a dance in the basement with a jazz band from New Orleans, wine by the barrel, and
free cigars. Finally in my declining years I've seen the light. All of
that is *good,* really, and the good Lord wouldn't want us to deny the
pleasures of life to our poor children."

Ben just chuckled. "And then we'll get Brother Detweiler in for a
seminar on the eschatological passages of the Gospel of Mark, and
he'll explain to everybody that the tribulation will start two weeks
from tomorrow and we might as well quit feeding the stock and stay
inside and pray."

"Or else flee to the mountains when we see the desolating sacri-
fice set up," I said, "whatever that might be. Ah, Ben, it'd be easier if
it were the End Times, wouldn't it? Then we could stop all this wrangling about doctrine and modernism and fundamentalism and just
let things happen."

"And get some rest, right?"

"And get some rest." Here was Clara with a plate of cookies and a
glass of lemonade for herself. "And how have your folks been?" Ben
asked her.

"Getting along; they both had the grippe in January, but they've
been well since. Papa is still leading prayer meeting every month or

so, and they like it here. Mama says she doesn't miss cooking and cleaning one bit." Clara paused. "How are things in town?"

"Oh, about the same." We all looked out across the yard for a while; the rain had washed the air clean and everything looked crisp and green and beautiful. Even the fallen limbs with their new leaves hadn't faded yet. "I don't know what's going to happen if we get into this war with Hitler, though. I thought we'd had enough war to last us a lifetime, but I'm afraid this one will be even worse than the last. And just when the others in town seemed to be forgetting about us being German."

"What will your church's boys do, if there's another war?" Clara asked.

"That's a question," Ben said. "I don't even know what my own boys will do. They were talking around the table about joining the navy, the other night. I have talked about nonresistance and being in the world but not of it till they know what I'm going to say better than I do, but they aren't convinced yet."

"I think it's time to get the peace sermon out again, George," Clara said, "the one that says you can't see how anybody who professes to be a Christian can get the idea that it is right to kill a fellow man."

I knew the one she meant. "It doesn't seem that long since I preached it," I said. "I've been through that one often enough that I almost have it by heart. 'We hear this remark so often the man that is not willing to die for his country isn't fit to be a citizen. I would say the one that is not willing to die for the principles of Christ is not a citizen of his eternal Kingdom.' It doesn't seem there's much doubt when you put it that way, does it?"

Ben was studying the chips of ice left in his glass. "But what do we do, George, when some of our flock do choose to go to the war? Do we cut them off once and for all, so that they turn to the Methodists or the Lutherans for their spiritual needs—or just stay home on Sunday and read the papers? What should I do if my boys join the service, whatever I might say to them?"

"Any father that would not stand with his child is cruel," Clara said, "no matter what they may do. It's God's place to judge—ours is to love, our neighbors and our enemies and our sons." Then she stopped and took a drink, and I knew she was thinking what I was: that it was one thing to say so, but another to stand face to face and have to do it. "How many of our Meadows boys do you think will join the army, George?"

"I hope we can persuade most of them to stay out of the service," I said. "It seems there may be better chances for them to do some kind of other work, not carrying guns, if we do get into it again. I think our Don will not go, from what he's said, and Gerdon is too old and has children already. But there are a lot in the church who listen to the radio and read the papers, and they've heard over and over that whatever it might take to stop this Hitler has to be done and that it's not fair of us to expect others to fight while we stay home safe and sound. Then there are the ones that think Hitler's German like them and not so bad, no matter how many little countries he gobbles up . . ."

"I remember Papa telling about Father Stuckey," Clara said, "saying that he always said that putting a member aside was like tearing a branch from the tree, that it would wither and die and be good only for the fire. Why, Father Stuckey never even wanted to set back that Schoolteacher Joder, for all his wild ideas."

"I used to see old Joder when I was a boy," I said, "riding into town to pick up his mail. There was a stern old man. To look at him you'd think he never had a new thought in his life, as serious and respectable as he looked . . . well, except for the pipe, and that he'd shaved his beard. People would point him out and whisper about him as though he had killed and eaten his children, but he was gentleman enough to me, though a mite severe. He stopped me once to see how my German was and gave me a licorice whip when he found I could at least say 'Guten Tag, Schulmeister' without stumbling all over. He told me that I should work on my accent and my vocabulary and that he'd test me again the next time we met, but not long after that he died. I never saw that he meant any harm to anyone, except for spreading that universalist nonsense."

Ben laughed all at once, the sort of laugh that comes when you're surprised and pleased by your life turning a little richer than you expected. "Here we started out with Reverend Strubhar and we're all the way back to Schulmeister Joder," he said, "with Hitler and Father Stuckey in between. What next?" And we laughed with him for a moment, and then of course both Clara and I remembered that he'd hardly come all the way out here just to chat with us about world events and the church fathers. And so we waited, knowing that it was just about time for him to get to it.

"I had a letter from Brother Hartzler this morning," he said. "It seems that our main speaker for the conference this year is showing some reluctance, and Brother Hartzler was hopeful that I might persuade him to take part."

"Oh, Brother Hartzler," I said. "And I'll bet he had nine different theories about my loss of confidence and then proceeded to beat each and every one to death with words of three syllables or more."

"No, only two or three theories. But you're right about the words."

Clara was surprised, I could see. I still hadn't said much to her about all of this; we'd been busy, but also I was pretty sure what advice she'd have for me—and I didn't especially want to hear it.

"Well, what's to say," I started, as much to her as to Ben. "I remember my father, when we were supposed to be out helping him and lagging back, wanting to slip off and play by the creek or just sit under a tree, saying that getting any work out of us was like trying to push a rope. That's how I feel about the whole deal these days. A man works himself night and day, trying to do the Lord's work for the old folks and the young and everybody in between, and all it gets him is complaints from the left and the right, straining over gnats and bickering over trifles. Here's a crazy German wanting to conquer the world, human blood running all over Europe like slaughtering day on the farm, and here we are quarreling over pageants on the church platform and how we're going to find two hundred dollars to put a roof on a building. The old men are stubborn and the young ones are worse, Ben, and you and I are stuck in the middle of it, with all of them convinced that if we aren't fools we're ignorant. Well, let them wrangle it out for themselves. I've had my fill of it."

Very rarely did I speak for so long at a stretch, except from the pulpit, and both Ben and Clara were impressed enough by that not to answer me right away, though I did see them sneak a look at each other. Ben took a long drink of what was left of his lemonade and picked up a cookie. Clara got up and went inside, and for a moment I thought she was angry at me too, which more or less would have suited the mood I was in. But she was just checking on her cookies; in a minute I heard her feet on the stairs again.

"Well, there's one batch for the pigs!" she said, shaking her head. "If I'd have know you were going to deliver such a sermon I'd have set the timer to remind me."

She sat back down and we all stayed there a little longer. It was getting toward suppertime, and looking south from the porch in the golden light we could see right out past the home yard and the houses of Meadows village, out into the open fields. I could just see the roof of the church, at the other end of town, and beyond it the hard road where a few cars were moving. The corn was just coming up, the spring wheat hand-high already, and all sorts of birds were fluttering around, making noise and nests and whatever all it is that birds do.

"Papa took us back to the cabin where he was born once," Clara said, "in the timber by Rock Creek. He loved to tell how rough that place was, how the wolves howled in the winter and the boys in the loft woke up with snow on their comforters of a chilly winter morning. Of course we girls thought it was so romantic, all hidden away back there, rough logs with daubing between them and a door with a latch string, just two tiny windows, and nothing but a fireplace for heat and to cook on. By then nobody was living there and it was falling apart—I'm sure it's gone by now. But it was a start, that cabin and that patch of woods. Grandpa Strubhar made enough money on that walnut grove and sawmill to buy the good farm out on the prairie—well, you know that. And the Washington church wasn't even there then, nor this church, hardly a decent road even. The prairie was so wide and wild that Uncle Christian got lost coming home from town with the wagon and spent most of the night under the stars before they found him, and him only twelve years old. And Great-Grandma Marie came all the way over here to settle in a cabin that didn't even have a floor."

I had heard these stories before, but I held my peace, knowing that Clara was working up to something and that when she took this much time doing it I had better pay attention.

"From wherever you are, your problems look bigger than anybody else's," she said, "and the work that's there for you to do looks harder and less appealing. Would you like to trade with me for a while, George? There are days when I think that I'll scream if I have to mangle one more pair of pants or melt if I have to stand in the steam and take one more batch of green beans out of the canner. There are days when I don't know how I will manage to be nice and sweet and Christian toward the old folks, even the ones that deserve it. I tell you what. Maybe you and me should just trade. I dare say I could get up in front of people and read the Bible and pray and talk through my hat for the better part of an hour, though I suppose there'd be those somewhat surprised if I did it."

Clara was getting wound up herself, now. "Or we could just retire, make up bundles, and hit the road. The train comes through town twice a day. I bet Colorado is nice this time of year. If we left the car behind we'd save on gas. Wouldn't you like to see the Rockies before we die? We could be there in three days, if not less. Gerdon's out on his own and Don's almost grown anyway, they'd get by without us. And the church did its business before we came. Somebody would take over with the old folks. They'd all get along without us."

I found myself imagining what she'd said, just getting on the train with a suitcase and whatever money we could scrape together, heading off to see the world. For a moment I really thought we'd do it, get out from under everything and never have to worry again.

When my head cleared from that one, I started wishing Clara could preach the sermon, just to hear what she'd say and how some of the old folks would take a woman preaching, and almost missed the last of what she said with imagining it. And I thought, not for the first time, that if I'd been born half as smart as Clara I could have been president. She might have just come right out and said what we both knew was true, that if I weren't so mule-headed and prideful I would save us both a lot of trouble and the church besides. But she always had some story or other, something that nibbled around the edges of the problem until what was left didn't seem such a big thing to handle.

Ben could see I was weakening, and he set down his empty glass. "George, you need to think about where you are, in between the college boys and the old men. We all need somebody like you to keep us all talking, to show us we shouldn't bust ourselves into pieces every time we get crosswise over some trifle. Lord knows there have been splits and schisms enough.

"Why not take it straight on, talk about the need for confidence and sticking to the job at hand? If you're feeling uncertain, you know others are too. Help us to see our way through the doubts and the wrangles, to get back to what matters. When the war comes, we'll need all the unity we can find."

Ben talked on, about the good things that had come out of the conference, about the promising young people he knew, about how men like us needed something to fill up our spare time anyway. And I sat there with my arms crossed on my chest, muttering and grumbling a little, and then the talk turned to the planting, which had gone very well for once, and the tornado south of us that had torn up a bunch of farms, and after awhile Ben said he had to be getting along and Clara said, "Surely you'll stay for supper." So he came out with me to the barn for chores and I started in on the milking while he scattered hay in the troughs, just like we'd been doing it all our lives, which of course we had.

George did preach in the end, on August 19, 1938, at Tremont, Illinois. According to the **Conference Yearbook** *for 1939, "He stressed the need of our rising to God's standards, rather than toning His standard down to our level, even though to do so may mean bearing the cross. Our service is to be rendered in one spirit, the spirit of Christ, and for one purpose, the salvation of souls, for Christ and the Church."*

It's a blessing to ponder such a moment near the end of a project like this, four years spent harrowing back and forth through these materials both scanty and surfeiting, too little and not enough, trying to feel my way into these people and knowing that the best I can do is fake it convincingly. I can see George on the platform set up in a hot tent, his full, solid frame and shock of graying hair, all his pastorly authority gathered around him, pleading one more time for a rising to God's standards. Did he truly recover his confidence, find himself granted a shining, lasting vision of the great things his people would do? Or was it all a charade, going through the motions and hoping no one could see his inner emptiness? Was he somewhere between, where I always seem to find myself, caught in a maze of convictions, blazing certainties, raving doubts, until I'm hard put to say on any given day just who I am, much less what my personal theology might be? And what did Clara truly think about it all? Her diary for the day reads only, "Conference began. Small crowd but good talks. Stayed at Rev. Miller's all night. Hot."

I don't know, and nobody I've asked has any idea, and once again I suspect nobody left on this vale of tears is going to settle the question for us. And finally, I think, why he did it doesn't matter so much. It's the act that matters, and if it's done with all sorts of impurities and doubts, well, that's not exactly unusual.

Running under this whole story, mostly unstated until now, has been another one: the story of my encounters with the more skeptical circles of contemporary theory. As I worked and lived with George and Clara, reading in the literary magazines I subscribe to started to feel like being suddenly teleported from the earth to the moon. I would emerge from their enormous web of relationships—church people, relatives, neighbors, friends—to read opinions like this one, from the critic Donald Revell: "The tension and the sad beauty of contemporary satire arise from a nostalgia for community experienced even as the poet comes to understand that community is a desperate fiction capable of great viciousness in the defense of its folly against the witness of individuality."

Revell is smart and knowledgeable and skillful, so I will not say that this is simply wrong. But after my days with George and Clara, it certainly feels wrongheaded. Communities are "capable of great viciousness," of course, and always a fiction if we claim some absolute goodness or authority for them. The larger they are, the more dangerous their follies, and my nostalgia for that Meadows community is tempered by the near certainty that I would have found it a fairly stuffy place to live. Yet surely the fiction of community is not always desperate and not always vicious. How can Revell claim that all communal experience is mere foolishness? And aren't desperation and viciousness more likely to arise from a self-defensive individuality?

*Revell goes on to say, "It is heroism (in minor keys, in the studious ges-
tures of disillusionment) that continues to fill circles of absence with new
poems. All distances imply death, as every object that recedes from sight
implies an ultimate abandonment." And again I find my brow wrinkling
at the distance between this and what I take to be the true and the real. If
we begin to call "studious gestures of disillusionment" "heroic," just what
is our language worth? Am I deluded to find these sentences full of self-
pity and a weird inverted arrogance, an enormous and unexamined belief
in disbelief? The first counterstatement that occurred to me, "All distances imply life, as every object that recedes from sight implies an ultimate
homecoming," is obviously a statement of faith. And, if we were truly trying to level with the universe, wouldn't we want something like "All distances imply the processes of nature going on without us, as every object
that recedes from sight implies that we are limited but the cosmos is not"?*

*George made his gesture of disillusionment, but even in doing so what
he saw around him were not "circles of absence" but a people and a world
living and breathing and carrying on the complicated, confused, mistake-
filled conversations of life. He saw himself as part of a community, however minor and marginal and fallen it was, and knew that what he did
mattered to others, if only a few. And finally he found his confidence, or
something like it, and went on with the work.*

*We could discuss here, I suppose, what it means to be heroic. In an ad-
equately flowery and turgid eulogy for George, his fellow preacher William
Weaver wrote, "Some one has said, 'he who is conscious of a debt he can
never pay, will be forever paying it.' And so we are greatly indebted to our
brethren who have gone before, and it brings to us the sobering sense of
responsibility for those who are gone as well as for those who are to come."
For Weaver, as for George, the idea that absence is more real than presence, that isolation is more basic to human life than community, must
have seemed too odd, too incongruous with experience and tradition, to
deserve serious thought. Their deep sense of themselves as part of a historical process, part of a group with both a past and a future, gives their
work weight and substance—and makes me think that to point out their
simplicity, their awkwardnesses, their lack of sophistication, while all those
things are apparent, is almost irrelevant, like criticizing the bees for the
clumsiness and noise of their flying instead of tasting the honey.*

7. MURPHY

Murphy thought he'd seen and heard it all, worked in the mud
and ice and heat, carried block and brick and laid them both, mixed
mud and hauled it, gone to bed too tired to wash his face in four

different states. This job was nothing so different, bigger than some, smaller than others: an addition to the Old People's Home in Meadows, a tiny little town with one store and one church, an elevator, a post office, and two dozen houses. The preacher and his wife lived in the home and did everything from keeping the books to cooking and cleaning to holding the old folks' hands when they were sick or crazy; the preacher kept disappearing in a beat-up truck, coming back hours later with it full of hay or straw or sweet corn. When he wasn't out somewhere he spent most of his time checking up on Murphy and his crew, so Murphy didn't mind.

There was some money from their church and some others to get this addition started, although not much extra from the way they had the whole project shaved right to the bone. They did pay Murphy and the rest prompt and every penny they owed, every Saturday noon, so that part was all right. Still, Murphy thought as he climbed the scaffold for the first time that day, a man laying brick who can't swear might just as well have his good right hand stiff as a brick itself and no more use to him but as a weight to haul around.

The old man was friendly enough otherwise, plenty used to hard labor and not so picky that he didn't see quick enough that Murphy worked hard and well and put up with no slacking from his boys, either. The wife was generous with the iced tea and cookies when the day got hot and long. But it was the second day in the morning, the dew just drying off the brick, when Murphy dropped one on his thumb and hopped around holding it and carrying on to ease the pain. His father used to tell him there was no good to be gained by swearing unless the object of your wrath had ears to hear you, but Murphy had found over the years that a good long string of abuse had a surprising way of taking his mind off his problems. By the time he'd finished, if he was lucky and got on a strong roll, he would be almost so pleased with himself for not stumbling or repeating anything that he could forget what had gone wrong and get back at it.

So this morning was nothing so special; Lord knows he always had a thumb or a finger black and blue. And he let a little streak loose, not so much by his standards, but enough that George straightened up from where he was mixing mud and gave Murphy a long hard look. He muttered something and went for a bandage and thought nothing of it.

They made good progress over the next week, with the weather holding at hot and dry. One afternoon somehow the Lord's name worked its way into the conversation as Murphy was telling young Smith for the third time that he needed brick today, not in time for church on Sunday. And the next day as they were cleaning up he could not help observing that a girl who was passing had a fine healthy set of attributes upon her. Murphy knew from talking to George that he was a farmer and had kept cattle most of his life, so he didn't see that he'd have any objection to discussing the qualities of fine flesh, animal or human. But he could see George go a little red under his summer tan.

They must have spent two hours painting that night, tired as they always seemed; they used two of the two by eights from the scaffold, and did a nice neat job of it too, with letters a foot tall if they were an inch and the whole thing ten feet long where they had nailed it to the scaffold. "Swear Not At All," it said, with the passage from Matthew or wherever it may be in smaller letters at the end. It was the damndest sight Murphy had ever seen on a job, and he almost dropped his lunch pail as he stood there looking at it.

Well a man ought to control himself, I have always said, don't get me wrong I know that it's not easy. And so as we sat there at supper, talking about the work that was going well enough and the language that kept floating through the windows as she cleaned and ironed and made preserves, words I declare and Clara would affirm she had reached this ripe old age and never heard from me, she hit on the idea of making a sign. While she was washing up I hunted up some paint—red it was, fitting enough it seemed—and a brush that would serve and laid out two of the extra planks that they'd brought for scaffolding.

I was done with "Swear" and working on "Not" when she came out to see how it was going. She was so pleased that she grabbed me from behind and practically spilled the paint, which I set down long enough to give her a hug back and admire my handiwork. Then she had to hunt up her own brush so she could help, and she did the big "All" at the end and the chapter and verse below in smaller letters while I worked toward her. We carried it outside with the paint still wet and put it up on the scaffold where the men could not miss it first thing in the morning. I used sixteen-penny spikes to fasten it solid; I didn't want them to think it was just a passing whim of ours.

We were up earlier than ever the next morning, and Clara was like a schoolgirl, giggling and peeking out the window as we waited for the men to come. The first as usual was Murphy, the crew boss and the worst mouth of them all, though I must admit that I myself could not work harder nor lay a straighter wall. He spotted the sign right off and came to a dead stop. Through the window we could see his eyes go narrow as he read it slowly, and his face, which was always red from the sun—and, no doubt, from the booze he drank in the evenings—went one shade redder and then another. And then he just stood there—I suppose it was only a minute, but it seemed forever. Finally he moved off toward the big tree where he always left his lunchpail, but slowly, as though someone had knocked him in the head with a stick and he was still recovering.

I decided it was time to greet him, so I ambled out the door. He straightened up from putting down his pail and saw me coming, and the look that crossed his face I hope I never forget. Good morning, I said, or something such, and he chuckled a little, and said, "Yes, good morning, George. You must have had a long night of it."

"Oh, not so long," I said. "And for some reason I slept like a baby."

"That right?" he said. "I slept well enough myself, considering the heat."

"Yes, it promises to be another scorcher," I said, and then paused. I was sorely tempted to seize the moment for a little speech about how cool and soothing even this day would seem beside the fires of hell, where the very flesh would burn and not be consumed. But just as I was gathering myself Murphy looked at me hard with those squinty, bleary, tough old eyes of his, and so I just waited.

He seemed to be waiting for his own words to come. From the look on his face I didn't know whether to expect an apology or another string of profanity and an offer to quit on the spot if I didn't think the tender ears of Meadows could stand such talk.

"We're nearly up to the second floor windowsills," he said finally. "We can run stone below the frames or brick right up to them, but I'll need you to come up with me and see what looks best to you. If you want stone we'll have to call the yard this morning."

It was the longest speech without an un-Christian word in it that I'd ever heard from him. "I like the look of stone, myself," I said, "if it's not too high. What would you do?" He started into the details and we went off to the scaffold, his blunt scarred fingers poking the air as he explained the options to me. Every few words he paused, sometimes just for a flash, sometimes longer, and sometimes he gulped as though he was swallowing the words that he knew I didn't want to hear. I heard him out and asked some questions, and we decided the stone would be best.

As we came down from the scaffold the other men were just arriving. Of course they could hardly miss the sign, and I must admit I almost had to laugh at the way they stood and gawked and looked over at me and then hung their heads like schoolboys who've been caught making trouble at recess. Murphy was ready for them, though. "Well, men?" he yelled. "Do you think the work will get done by studying it all day?" They started moving then, and I started back inside to call the yard about the stone. I heard him muttering under his breath as I went, but I couldn't quite pick up the words.

The first sweat of the day was on Murphy's forehead. Not a cloud anywhere, just that pale haze that means muggy and miserable. Hotter than the hubs of hell, he thought, hot enough to scorch the Devil's tail. What's this old world coming to, he thought, when a man can't even speak his mind out loud for fear of offending some old woman's tender ears? Stone would look good for the windowsills, though. A good week's work left, maybe closer to two, and then on to the hospital in Pontiac, with a little job or two in between. His helper dumped a batch of mud behind him, splashing it over on Murphy's pants as he did every time, and Murphy looked at him and started to speak and then saw the look in the boy's eyes and just laughed, knowing there was really nothing he needed to say.

8. GEORGE AND CLARA

The stories and words of other people have echoed and reverberated all through these pages. Many of them have been preserved thanks to Hilda Troyer, whose husband, Lotus, succeeded George at the Meadows church. In the seventies she worked for what must have added up to years on a biography of George and Clara, though eventually she gave it up, worn down by the effort and the uncertainties of publication. When she found out I was starting into this project, she told me to come over to her duplex in Meadows and gave me a whole grocery bag full of stuff. She had letters, clippings, notes, and hundreds of pages of drafts; sometimes I found five or six versions of the same pages, each just a few words different, but other sections had been drastically rewritten as she found more or better information.

I have spent more time sniffing around in Hilda's materials, and found more behind-the-scenes tidbits there, than in any other single source. She clearly loved George and Clara, with a devotion that gets almost embarrassing at times; she was the one who announced in 1976, when the Meadows home proclaimed Clara Queen for a Day, "Clara Gundy, you are a saint!"

This book might exist without her work, but not in the form that it has now. So it seems only right to let Hilda speak in her own voice for a little while. Here is a brief passage from her manuscript.

George and Clara at Home

"Come in! Come in!" (No one could mistake the quality of that invitation—it is persuasive and the emphasis is on *come*.) The invitation is at once a greeting and a command. There is a squeak of a rocking chair in the interior of the house, and the rustle of a morning paper, at your rap on the screen door of the little white frame house Clara and George selected for retirement in Meadows, Illinois. With hair slightly rumpled, George is smiling as eager anticipation lights his face. His half-curved arm (with long shirt-sleeves stopped midway by rubber sleeve holders) reaches and grasps your shoulder, as he guides you through the doorway into the living-room.

George's face is radiant, as it so often is when happy, excited about something or genuinely pleased. He seats you in the most comfortable chair in the room, as a gesture of kindness, consideration, and a place of special privilege. You are somewhat overwhelmed by all this attention and search for a way to begin the conversation.

The smell of new cloth attracts your attention and you see a freshly marked quilt carefully covered and stored in the corner of the room. George seats himself quietly, and waits for your composure, meanwhile watching you quietly and openly, just observing your interest in the quilt. "The women (meaning his wife and the ladies of the church), are starting a new quilt." Just a statement of fact, no resignation or half-drawn sigh escaped.

At that moment Clara came into the room, wiping her hands on her apron. "It's an applique quilt," Clara said. She is so tall, and so thin! Her face is lined, and she is perspiring behind her glasses. "It's going to be hard to do . . . such heavy material." Clara chats on about quilts, and as she chats and George listens, you feel the combined love these two people have for you.

Somehow, without being noticed, Clara leaves the room from time to time, but returns in time to enter into the gaiety, or the punch line. Time slips away, until you find yourself led (you do not know how it all came about) to a place at the family table, fresh with a white linen cloth and fragile china. Reality comes back to you with a flash when Clara hands you a platter of top-of-the-stove fried chicken, followed in quick succession by a dish of fluffy white mashed potatoes, a boat of chicken gravy, a dish of green peas dotted with butter, garden lettuce with cream, sugar and vinegar dressing, (if lucky a jar of home-made tomato jam) sliced bread with real butter, followed with ground cherry pie and hot coffee. I don't believe the most confirmed food faddist could refuse one speck of Clara's superb meal. The final touch: balls of ice cream in a serving dish, fresh from the freezer.

When the meal is over, the dishes done, the garden checked, or the new plants in the window, or a gift from one of the children examined, remorse and embarrassment set in. You are ashamed because of the extra effort on the part of your hosts. You are embarrassed because of your inability to refuse the generously proferred hospitality. As you leave, two quarts of freshly picked berries or grapes are tucked in by your feet. As you drive away, amazed and incredulous, you vow to never again impose on such wonderful people, but you know in your heart the vow will be broken. A visit to the Gundy's always ends this way for every human being that steps up the three short steps to the porch and raps on the door with the glass window framed with a coarse lace net curtain. After you enter the door, you are not in control, your sense of reason and timeliness flee. You find yourself in a world apart where love, affection and empathy overcome your worldly judgment. Helplessly you succumb.

I remember those balls of ice cream; at home we always just scooped it out of the carton. Being just a kid during my own dinners at George and Clara's—it was just Clara by then—I had nothing like Hilda's sense of half-guilty hero worship. I was just brought there, told where to sit and to be quiet while the prayer was said. Clara would make a roast, trim the fat off and put it on her plate, and then pass the rest around. She'd make noodles with cornflake crumbs on top when we came, because my father liked them. She'd drink a cup of hot water, plain, for dessert, while we kids fidgeted until we were set free and could scramble outside to play.

Anywhere in Meadows seemed legal to us; there were patches down by the tracks where the kinds of weeds that dried long and straight and with hardly any roots grew, and we pulled them out and threw them like spears. The best times were when my first-cousins-once-removed Duane and Ralph were there, because they were such wild guys and thought everything was fine as long as we didn't die doing it. Sometimes they brought a BB gun, once even a .22 I think, and we shot it at a makeshift target down by the tracks, taking turns, counting shots.

When they weren't there I was usually bored, the oldest of the great-grandchildren, too young for the adults and too old for my brothers and sisters and whoever else was there. I sniffed around her books, looking for something exciting. All I remember finding was one called **Epidemic,** *in which the only racy scene occurred when a sailor came to see a loose woman who "knew that below the neck she could compare herself to anybody" or some such. He passed on the plague to her, naturally, and then all heck broke loose.*

So we'd pour her button collection out on the floor and look through it, showing the odd ones to each other. She had thousands, I suppose, and my mother still has a batch of the green ones sewn onto a card hanging in her hallway. We'd hide each other in the trunk upstairs, which was not particularly exotic or antique but plywood covered with cloth patterned in blue, black, and yellow. Downstairs in a corner of the front room was the old rolltop desk, crammed with all sorts of papers and junk I remember rooting around in halfheartedly as a child, but would give who knows what to be able to look through again now. It was the main attraction when Clara had her sale and went to the home to live, in 1967. I got a little hairbrush as a keepsake and had it through my college years, but lost track of it somewhere.

9. CLARA

I never really slept in church, not near so much as people said, anyway. Oh, my eyes would slip shut, now and then, and I'd drift a little away from George's preaching, not that he wasn't always biblical and interesting too, but after thirty or forty years a body comes to learn some things about what to expect next. And there weren't many other times for me to just sit and think, without something to occupy my hands, at least, if not my mind too. So I'd find myself getting comfortable even on the hard bench and not stirring to stop Don or Ralph when they were little, even when I knew one or the other had turned around to make faces at the people behind us. I'd be in another place somehow, where the past and the present and things that had never happened and never would were all there, not jumbled exactly, neat enough, just all *together,* and so many of them that I could content myself with just wandering about, looking and listening and smelling, even while I could still hear George's voice with part of my mind and the boys' little noises with another.

So there I'd be, back in Grandma Strubhar's kitchen, with those eight tall kerosene lamps all lined up in the wooden sink on the west side of the kitchen, wicks trimmed, chimneys washed, and Grandma bustling about getting them lit and set about for us to see by in the parlor and the dining room, all while she was making gravy and grating cabbage for cole slaw and making sure the table was set just right. It never was any use to tell her to sit down and take it easy; she'd run as much as walk, Sundays, just to be sure that everyone was fed and happy. When her time came, she told us she was going to die and not to bother with the doctor because she'd lived eighty years and evidently the Lord thought that was enough. And sure enough, she didn't last the night. After her funeral we came back to the house and ate bread she'd baked the Saturday before.

Or I'd see my sisters, Ada and Lucy, both of them taken away before they'd more than just begun to live. Ada was never very strong, but when Papa got the schoolteacher to stop by and pick her up on his horse each day, I thought she was awfully lucky and wondered why I didn't get to ride up there too, with those strong arms wrapped around me. But she never made much of it, only told me that he had bad breath and his coat scratched her. I dared her one day to carve her name in a board on the porch, and she started it, but then we got called in to set the table and forgot about it, and it was only after she'd gone that we found what she'd done, "ADA STRU," just like her life itself, cut short in the middle.

And what could I ever say about Lucy? She was the brightest and quickest of us all, plenty sassy but not mean, just always ready to go. I guess I was about eleven when they brought her home from Uncle Joseph's that terrible day, all wrapped up and covered with bandages and shrieking, nothing like the child who'd left to play with her cousins that morning. When Mama and Papa had settled her in the front room Papa sat us all down at the table, and I've never seen his face so dark and crumpled looking. "Lucy's dress caught fire," he said, "while she was jumping over the ashes of a fire she and Chester and Phoebe thought was out. She got scared and ran, and that just made it worse. Phoebe tried to put the flames out, but . . ." Papa put his hands over his face and rubbed his eyes. Lucy moaned from the other room.

She was with us for a week more, never really clear-headed, sunk so deep in her pain that she couldn't sleep or eat or talk or do anything but cry out. It was as though she was searching for the right sounds, the right call, the one that would set her free. At last she found it.

Oh, we had our losses, all right. Ralph, our middle son, was just sixteen when the car he was riding on got hit by a train in Chenoa. It was lunch hour at school, and he and his friends were in the habit of riding uptown to a restaurant for a bite of this or a nibble of that to round out the school lunches. George and I had gone to Chicago that day for a meeting at Moody's and no more than got there, with the roads slippery with ice all the way, than we got word he'd been hurt and we'd better go home fast. That was a terrible journey home, with George leaned over the wheel, wanting to go sixty but not daring, both of us frantic with the traffic and the ice and the worry. And when we got to Pontiac somebody was waiting there by the side of the road to stop us and take us to the hospital where he was lying, so still and quiet, not a mark on him except on one ankle. I thought he pressed back just a little with his hand once or twice, but that was all.

So it was easy enough to drift into such thoughts of a Sunday morning, all the bad and good I've seen. The boy driving the car when Ralph was killed turned out to be a drinker, and I often thought afterward, when it seemed so hard to give him up so young, that it would have been so much harder to see him be a drinker. I guess God knows best. Ralph and Bill Gittinger and Herbert Roszhart were building a clubhouse in our yard, but after Ralph was gone they never worked on it again.

One Sunday right after Christmas I was startled when a man burst into the sanctuary right in the midst of the sermon. "The Rosenbergers' is on fire!" he yelled. George right away sent the men out to help and went himself; after a bit of looking at each other, and seeing that there were plenty to watch over the children, some of us women went out too, but by the time we got there the place was started pretty good and there were so many men going in and out that we could see any more would just be in the way. The Rosenbergers were gone to church, but the door was open and the fire started upstairs, so before it spread too far they managed to bring out the rugs, the curtains, most of the china and silverware, and as many clothes and photos and suchlike as they could. They even got the Christmas presents and the tree from the living room. It made quite a pile, all of that stuff put down in a scramble in the snow. Finally the flames got too hot to go back in, and I found George to be sure he was all right, and just about then the fire department from Gridley finally came. George went with them to show where they could get water from the cistern at the home, but it was too late for them to do much but wet down the houses next door to keep them safe.

I'd seen plenty of brush piles burn before and even a barn once or twice. But it was something to stand there in the cold, with just an inch of snow on the ground and the sky clear and sharp, and watch the second-biggest house in town burn right to the ground. The thing I didn't expect was just how pretty it all looked, in a crazy sort of way, with those big orange-golden flames wrapping themselves up around the windows and the big plumes of black smoke sailing off against the blue sky and the smell of burnt oak and the rattling sounds of the burning. We all just stood there and watched it go, cold on our backs but our front sides warmed by the fire. What a world, I thought, where we get warm by watching somebody's home go up in smoke. We work and struggle all our lives to build a place of our own and then maybe go off to church one Sunday and come home to find it just a smoking heap, with the Christmas presents and the rugs and the good china stacked up out in the snow, under the open sky.

For once we didn't have company for dinner that Sunday. We had to drive to Chicago to visit someone in the hospital, so George told the Rosenbergers they were welcome to stay at our place for a few days. They said thanks, but they had relatives at Weston and thought they would sooner be out of town for a while, at least until the ash that was all over town got blown away or covered with new snow. Still they couldn't seem to stop thanking George for his help in saving their things, long after he was embarrassed and getting gruff, telling them it was nothing so heroic, that anyone would have done the same.

We'd been in our own home less than a year then, and the thought ran through my mind that whatever our losses, at least we'd never been burned out. Not that I'd trade any one of the people we'd lost for a house, but still it was something. I said as much to George in the car, and he nodded, with his hands propped on the wheel, in that little slouch he drove with when the road was clear. He didn't say anything really, but I knew he was thinking about the morning, about stopping in midsermon to save the worldly goods of a neighbor. When he finally looked over at me he had that glint in his eye.

"Best sermon I ever preached, anyway," he said.

"Lay not up treasures on earth," I said. "Right?"

"I was thinking more, 'Love thy neighbor as thyself.' Or, turn off the space heaters when you go off to church."

I couldn't help but laugh. "You're a hard man, George Gundy," I said, "and you've preached long enough to know that there's nothing biblical about space heaters. Next you'll be drawing some lesson out of the Christmas presents, I suppose."

He laughed too. "Well, I was thinking . . ." Then he went quiet for a little. "Any time but Sunday, if the place had caught fire, they might have been home. They might have caught it in time to put it out and nothing hurt. Or they might have all gone up with the place."

I'd been thinking about that too. "And surely there wouldn't have been a hundred men handy to save their things, any time except Sunday morning."

"God works in wondrous ways," he said, and we'd both heard him say that so many times that we laughed again, and then when we stopped we knew, again, how true and how wondrous it was.

One more quote, from Revell's commentary on the contemporary poet *Robert Hass:* "[His] satire rejects ethical community in favor of the terror that isolated hearts gratefully acknowledge as the subjectively beautiful, the aesthetic that may fix upon a particular . . . and elevate it to the level of a universal."

I want here to say hmm, as I do more and more in the margins of my students' papers. Revell makes no pretense of separating the "literary" and the life we all have to live, and so I suppose that I need not either. What sort of principle is it, then, to reject ethical community for isolated terror, even granted those moments of subjective beauty? Should we watch the house burn down because the flames look pretty, or should we try to save the Christmas toys? Is there no beauty within the community, in the gesture of the Mennonite pastor abandoning his sermon, sending the congregation out to save the worldly goods of a Baptist, dodging through the flames with an armful of packages? In the men assembling sweaty and sooty for a last prayer and then going home to retell the event over Sunday dinner? What sort of a world are we choosing to live in if we try somehow to reject community, given that we must continue to live in the contiguity, if not community, we all form in the most elemental and physical senses, no matter how isolated or alienated our subjectivity may tell us we are?

We may be alone in our minds, but in our bodies we are simply not. The web of quite actual physical and social relations that links us is sometimes gorgeous and sustaining; it is also, of course—and sometimes almost in the same moment—devastating and horrific. We should not idealize community, but we are not accurate if we imagine it does not exist.

10. CLARA

I'm feeling happy and anxious, knowing that my job may be just about finished, that I can print it all out and start thinking about something else, but also knowing how much isn't here, how many pleasing anecdotes and colorful stories I haven't managed to include, how much of the joys and pains of these lives will remain forever in the dark. I'm not sure that isn't for the best, some ways. I'm not sure if there's much to gain from telling the painful things I've skirted so far, most of them merely stories of how we get old and die. George had heart trouble for years, tried to retire but never really managed it, had various spells and illnesses. People at the church began to think it was time for new leadership, someone who'd be more in touch with the young people, more active. Hilda Troyer wrote that when he came to talk with her husband, Lotus, about taking over the *pastorate at Meadows, "George's face was white and drawn and his usually merry blue eyes were dull and pained. As the conversation continued and my husband accepted the call to go to Meadows, George straightened his posture and stated: 'Then I will tell the people at the Meadows church that they are your people now, and they must come to you for counsel and advice.' It was a broken and elderly man that left our home that day." He was seventy years old.*

George and Clara went to Fort Wayne not long after that, to help their son Don move to Woodburn, Indiana. George had a heart attack and lasted only five weeks, dying in Don's home on September 16, 1951. Clara wrote a long letter soon after to her grandson, Gerdon Jr.; he was off in boot camp, having joined the army as a medic.

Sept. 24, 1951.

My dear boy.

How I wish you could be working here at the Home now instead of where you are. I was so sorry you couldn't be at the funeral but I know just how hard it was for you to decide what to do and you can always remember the days you worked together. It was so nice you both could be there during the summer. He appreciated so much the fact that you boys didn't smoke or swear and if you can go on through your army life bearing that same testimony it will be a finer monument to Grandpa's teaching than all the memorials. You know his one ambition was that people would live Christian lives and that can only be done by reading God's Word. Never let a day go by but that you read some part of the Bible especially the New Testament. You will find Christian boys to associate with especially if you attend all the church services you can. I hope as the days go by you will get work to do of a constructive type rather than destructive. I pray for you every time I think of you and I need your prayers too. This whole experience seems like a horrible dream. Grandpa was a wonderful man always fine and clean in all his dealings and we have so many fine tributes to him in so many letters and cards, flowers, memorials and gifts.

Tuesday eve. there was a steady stream of callers. The screen door was never shut, people just kept coming. I shook hands with so many people my hand hurt. He looked so nice but was thin. He lost his appetite and food nauseated him. I tried to get him to eat a bite extra at first but tears would come in his eyes so finally I just gave him what he wanted and quit. One day he said "I don't believe I'm going to make it." I tried to tell him he had his year to finish out at church and how he could help next winter inside but he said "It will be a long time before I preach again." When Auntie Barb said good-bye to him last Sunday he told her "his work was done. The ministry is provided for and I'm ready to go."

We thought he was more alert on Sunday and after the folks left he slept. Don's wanted me to go to church and he wondered who would care for him if I went. I told Frances to go as I didn't want to leave him that long. He complained of pain in his back and I gave him a pill but he was sort of restless and used the urinal several times. He asked who was going to sleep with him and I told him I was. After I got to bed he felt he should get up so Don just came in the room and he said he would help him. That time he wanted on the slop jar. When he went to get up he said "I'm so sick," breathed hard 4 or 5 hard breaths and slumped in Don's arms. He got him on the bed and he was gone so quick.

I could see he was weaker and thinner every day but I just didn't think he wasn't going to get well. He had been through so many sicknesses and always came back but this time he had no reserve it seemed. Maybe he worked too long at the Home. It's so hard to go to church and see someone else where he always stood but Frank had a good talk on the "Unfinished Task" and reminded all of us of our part in finishing up the work. He never said much about Grandpa but he really did something for all of us. Lee Lantz preached a fine sermon and Lotus and Frank helped. The YPU quartet sang. There were about 800 at the church and 150 at the grave. It was so hard to leave him there but after all it was just his body. How I miss that whistle but Larry said as we left the grave, "In a couple of years you will get used to it." Time does heal our sorrow somewhat but we always miss those who are away. I was so thankful we had those 4 1/2 happy years in our own home.

I was so surprised to hear Lyle's voice over the phone Tues. morning. He is so much like Grandpa Strubhar. Aunt Ruth and Uncle Raymond came too. He went right back but Aunt Ruth went back with Don's yesterday. Dick, Jim and Donna went after Aunt Lina and the rest of us went to see Grandpa Gittinger. He was outside when we got there. We were at Roger's Friday night for supper, Don's, your folks and I. Arlene had such a nice meal. She is so sweet and they seem so happy, if only it won't be spoiled for them. Sat. night we were at Aunt Esther's for supper and Kay and kiddies were there. They came with a woman who was going to Chicago and didn't want to go alone. Uncle Harvey's and Aunt Ruth were there too and Aunt Ruth came back with us.

Tomorrow night the preachers are having a picnic at the Orphanage park and Frank's want us to go too. Wed. is Aid day and tonight your daddy is coming to help with sending off cards. Well I must close now and fix up the fire. It is rather cool in the house. The west side of the Old People's Home is about on. How I appreciate my two boys and all of you. My prayer is that you will all be *real* Christians.

With love   Grandma

After a long winter, Clara helped out the next summer at the confer-
ence church camp in Michigan. She cooked and cleaned, as usual, careful-
ly recording the numbers of campers in her diary—ninety-five one week,
sixty-five the next. She stayed in the first cabin that was built there, one
George had helped to frame and shingle the spring before. Forty years lat-
er the cabin is still there, and last summer, when my son went to camp
for the first time, he slept there too.

Clara would live on for twenty-seven more years, long enough to see
her oldest son die, long enough to see eleven grandchildren and dozens of
great-grandchildren come into the world. When she came out to our place
to help with one of the new babies, my mother hid ten dollars in Clara's
suitcase, knowing that she wouldn't take it from her hand. Clara bought
a dress for five dollars and sent the other five back with a note that said,
"Now we're both happy."

That may have been their gift, if anything was: to find those ways
through the world that make both sides happy, to be willing to settle for a
little themselves so that others could have a little too. It sounds sappy,
doesn't it? It's nothing new, particularly, not all that complicated, and not
unique. It has to do with that overburdened word **community***, a word I*
love and hate. George and Clara never expected to change the world in
any large way; their people have for centuries thought of themselves as a
remnant people, a few of the faithful in a world that would most certain-
ly remain fallen. The Anabaptist movement began, in the sixteenth cen-
tury, with the effort to free Christianity from the worldly entanglements
its members saw in both the Catholic and Protestant churches of their day.
The first Mennonites looked to reclaim the vision and practice of the early
church, especially its sense of separation from earthly powers, and they
saw the Emperor Constantine's institutionalization of Christianity as hav-
ing led to disastrous compromises of the teachings of Jesus. The true church,
they thought, might always be a small one; its task was not to be success-
ful in worldly terms, but to be faithful to the life and teaching of Jesus, to
support each other, and to do as much good in the world as they could
manage.

It seems to me that this sense of being a remnant is also a very useful
way of thinking about how we live in the world, whatever our religion.
We all despair, in greater or lesser ways, over the institutions we are linked
to, especially the largest and most energetically destructive ones. Yet we
also become connected over the years to an increasingly complex set of peo-

ple we rely on, trust, and consider at least worthy of being saved. They may be family, lovers, children, friends, colleagues, fellow poets, plumbers, auto mechanics; we may feel we have too few, or too many, or the wrong ones, but no one I know lacks such a personal community.

What many people seem to lack is a community of memory, one that extends backward in time, reminding them of where they came from, who their people have been, how they have struggled and blundered, suffered and persevered. As families scatter and dissolve, children live apart from parents and grandparents, the stories and traditions that preserve such a community of memory become harder and harder to maintain. Even in a family like mine, determined to maintain its memory, the job requires conscious effort, labor, and resources.

Much gets lost, no matter what we do. What we can salvage, piece together, reclaim, darned across the holes and thin spots, is not a whole story, not a complete set of answers to our questions. It won't give us a foundation safe from any tornado or earthquake, or a set of beliefs that no trial or disaster can shake. It won't provide a final, conclusive way of thinking about this stubbornly beautiful and terrible world.

But whatever our stance toward the world, it finally rests on one set of assumptions or another. We can choose one ready-made or try as Blake did to avoid that bondage by inventing our own, although that task is not for the fainthearted or the merely brilliant. Sooner or later, whatever our intelligence or our learning, we find our limits: we have no more hope of understanding whatever in the universe is more complicated than we are than rabbits have of understanding us. No matter what we think of Pascal's theology, he was surely right about the two infinities between which we exist. And it seems little more self-evident or convincing to me now to claim that death waits everywhere outside our vision, that estrangement is the fundamental human reality, that loss is the most important element of the human condition, than to calculate as Archbishop Ussher did that the world was created in 4004 B.C.

Years ago, when we were both in graduate school, I brought a friend into a composition class to have the students interview him—a real live poet. He gave a wonderful, provocative interview, though he more or less baffled the students, as I recall. I remember very clearly his assertion, "I don't believe in God. I believe in details."

This is a strong and even beautiful statement of a widespread view of the world, one that has yielded a great deal of good writing and some that I continue to find rewarding and even astonishing. I would not argue for its inverse—"I believe in God. I don't believe in details"—which is at least equally pernicious. And yet both of these senses of the world seem to me finally and radically poverty stricken. Wallace Stevens said, "The greatest poverty is not to live in a physical world," but isn't it an equal poverty to live in one that is merely physical?

I want to remain duly diffident here, both about my own beliefs and about passing judgment on others'. I don't know, in the first place, that what we believe is more than slightly a matter of choice. We all finally live inside our own heads and our own stories. I didn't choose George and Clara for my ancestors any more than they chose me, and given another set of ancestors I would certainly not be writing this particular book nor claiming this set of allegiances.

Yet I am grateful for having spent this time learning to know them (and the ones who came before them) better. I have discovered that they are mine, and I am theirs, in ways that it seems both foolish and uncharitable to ignore. It's not that I would trade my own set of ambiguities and resistances and murky affirmations for their apparent simplicity and confidence. I know that I don't want to give up movies and trashy literature and all the other things of the world to which I've grown accustomed. I hope they will understand, or at least forgive me.

And yet I am also glad to know that they are part of me, not only in the literal, physical sense but as a heritage I claim, models of one sort of worthy life to live. Their energy, their humility, their conviction, and their gentleness, their understanding of their work not as merely getting ahead or (worse) "finding" themselves, but as part of a larger enterprise, as furthering the life of the tribe, are things I yearn for as well. Hardest for me to claim is that sense of the work as not merely local, not just personal, but something ordained by the firm and present God who sees the little sparrow fall and numbers the (few) hairs on my head. And yet what do I know? Every fall in the pollen season my wife's bodily defenses go to red alert and flood her system with histamines and misery while I blunder mildly onward, breathing easily. I am reminded each time of how little my senses really deliver of what goes on. I am reminded to beware of claiming too much certainty of whatever kind; there's more going on than I can explain or understand. We may be surprised, overtaken, drowned, raptured—tomorrow or today.

Coda

How to end a story like this? George and Clara are gone, but their lives and deeds and even their physical presence shimmer on in hundreds of ways, through their descendants, the people they knew, the churches and organizations that they served. Once you know how to look for it, you see their signs everywhere, a set of eyebrows here, a turn of the head there, a habit of sitting easily, arms crossed, in a room filled with people talking, somehow making everyone a little easier. Stories that are told and retold, changing here and there, or recorded in obscure places where no one knows to look for them.

No real, human story can truly be finished off or summarized. They branch and tangle, dwindle and multiply, until they are not to be distinguished from each other, from all the other stories that are traveling on themselves into the unknowable future at one second per second.

***If I've told this story right**, I almost started, but I know that's a silly claim to make at the end of this book, at the end of this century. I haven't told it right, I haven't told "the truth," much less the whole truth. I've known too much or too little all along the way. The story as it's given here is only some fragments drawn from the tangled thicket of the past, tinkered and arranged and planted here for you like an imitation garden. It's not going to bear tomatoes or sprout wings or change into a butterfly. It's not objective and not fair, it's too kind to some people and too cruel to others, and it's my story as much or more than anyone else's, no matter how much I might protest.*

My telling is guilty and compromised in all the usual ways. My only excuse is that this human world is not objective either. Its true substance is not bodies and soil and homes and weapons, but thought and speech and memory: those things that flit through us while we are at rest or try-

ing to sleep or about some ordinary business. The true substance of the world is in those images, feelings, words that come back to us, memories that simply arise and linger, making no demands except that we acknowledge them, as real as any other piece of this terrible, humdrum, miraculous world.

There's a recent poem called "Meditation at Lagunitas," well known among those of us who read poems, by Robert Hass. It begins with these lines: "All the new thinking is about loss. / In this it resembles all the old thinking." The poem goes on to meditate about the inadequacy of language and to describe a woman the poet once loved, little things she did and said; he clearly wants to believe that such memories, and the placement of them in words, might somehow be enough, might give him solace:

> But I remember so much, the way her hands dismantled bread,
> the thing her father said that hurt her, what
> she dreamed. There are moments when the body is as numinous
> as words, days that are the good flesh continuing.
> Such tenderness, those afternoons and evenings,
> saying *blackberry, blackberry, blackberry.*

This is a poem that I love and cherish. Yet after all my days with George and Clara, I can't quite take it as the full gospel anymore. It seems too private, somehow, too convinced that nothing outside of romantic love and lyric emotion is really worth much. Maybe it's just the accident of my birth, the family I happen to have been dropped into. It's hard to explain, exactly. But every second or third year my branch of the Gundy family has a reunion at the camp George and Clara helped to get started. Now the brush has been cleared, or enough of it, and one of their grandsons is the facilities director. There are eighty-some of us, with the twenty-some cousins of my generation marrying and breeding our kind at a dizzying pace, so that by now the next generation, George and Clara's great-great-grandchildren, outnumber all the rest.

We stay in the comfortable lodges, take the kids swimming, walk the trails, and on Sunday morning we gather to sit together, report on our jobs and our children, reminisce and speak for the ages for an hour or so. My father always tries to say how humbled and impressed he is by what the next generation, my generation, has done and is doing. He's a fine farmer and a father I'm proud of, but a man not easy with words or in front of an audience, and he always ends up stumbling and then stopping. The words fail him, as they do all of us in the end, and he wipes his eyes a little and laughs a little and somebody else picks it up or somebody's child starts crying. But we know what he means to say. All the new thinking is not about loss.

It's 1964, January. I am eleven years old, and my grandpa and grandma and great-grandma have taken me with them to visit our relatives in Woodburn and Elkhart. I have never been away from home without my parents, and I'm almost overcome by the strangeness of it all, but I get to sit in front with my grandpa as he drives, and he tells me that I am in charge of the heat and should adjust it so that everyone stays comfortable. He has an almost-new Ford Galaxy, a nice car. I can't remember touching the heater controls, but maybe I do.

We get to Don and Fran's and I play with Duane and Ralph, their younger two boys, who are just about my age, wild and energetic guys who are great fun and dream up things I'd never think of doing. We play golf up and down the stairs and all over the house, using their dad's putter and a real ball and an indoor "hole" with little strips of metal that tip the ball up and into it if you hit it just right. We play Ping-Pong in the crowded basement and shoot baskets in the driveway after dark, with the porch light on. We go to church. Clara's diary says that Fran has just spent time in the hospital for a blood clot under her collarbone, but that's lost on me. I'm eleven, and she's just another slightly fussy mother. Never do I become aware that this is the house where George lived his last month, where he died.

The next day we drive on to Elkhart and my Uncle Dick's. His children are younger than me, and I don't have much to do. I lie awake what seems like all night in the bottom bunk of a strange bed, staring at the nightlight that my cousin Jon still needs. For supper, before that, my Aunt Jo made swiss steak. Clara was sitting next to me, and after the meat has been passed and we've all taken some she picked up almost all of hers and put it on my plate, with some quiet comment about how I needed it more than her. I didn't know what else to do, so I started in on it. There was a lot, more than I needed or wanted, tough enough that it had to be cut with a knife and chewed carefully, so that I was still working my way through it when everyone else was done. They looked at me, smiled, and said they were in no hurry. They went back to their grown-up talk, which I didn't pay much attention to. I smiled back, sort of, with my mouth full of meat, not knowing how to explain, just barely aware that I didn't need to.

I'm still a boy with too much meat on my plate, food that I didn't ask for or do anything to deserve. I am trying my best to finish it off, knowing that the others are glad they have been able to feed me but expect me to clean my plate. They hope I will keep the sauce off the tablecloth. They're kindly but they have standards, they keep track of what I'm doing even while they seem caught up in their grown-up conversation. All but Clara; she's right beside me, not saying much but taking in everything that happens. She has finished her own plate, having given most of her swiss steak to me, and refuses seconds but asks for a cup of hot water, plain. She takes small sips as I cut another bite of meat, put the knife down carefully on the edge of the plate, switch the fork to my right hand, and carry the bite to my mouth. It's not as hot as it was, but it's warm, swathed in tomato and onion, and it tastes good. I can feel her there, next to me, sipping her water, keeping the corner of her eye on me as she does on every one of us there in the room, not suspicious or angry, just hoping that we will be able to clean our plates, that there will be more to fill them when we need to eat again.

JEFF GUNDY is a native of the Illinois prairie where this book mainly takes place. His books of poems include *Inquiries* and *Flatlands*. His poems and essays have appeared in many magazines, including *Antioch Review, Exquisite Corpse, Georgia Review,* and *Ohio Review*. He has received two Ohio Arts Council fellowships and a C. Henry Smith Peace Lectureship. Since 1984 he has taught English at Bluffton College in Ohio.